904588

RESOURCE MATERIALS FOR TEACHERS

371.92
JOH
SL

D1080774

Epilepsy

This item is to be retu... st date
sta...
This iter...

A Practical Guide

Mike Johnson and Gill Parkinson

David Fulton Publishers
London

David Fulton Publishers Ltd
Ormond House, 26–27 Boswell Street, London WC1N 3JZ

www.fultonpublishers.co.uk

First published in Great Britain in 2002 by David Fulton Publishers

Note: The rights of Mike Johnson and Gill Parkinson to be identified as the authors of this work has been asserted by them in accordance with the Copyright, Designs and Patents Act 1988.

Copyright © Mike Johnson and Gill Parkinson 2002

British Library Cataloguing in Publication Data
A catalogue record for this book is available from the British Library.

ISBN 1–85346–829–0

All rights reserved. No part of this publication may be reproduced, stored in a retrieval system or transmitted, in any form, or by any means, electronic, mechanical, photocopying, recording or otherwise, without the prior permission of the publishers.

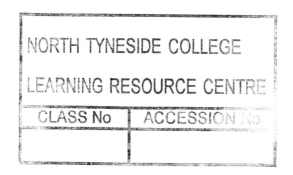

NORTH TYNESIDE COLLEGE

LEARNING RESOURCE CENTRE

CLASS No	ACCESSION No

Typeset by Mark Heslington, Scarborough, North Yorkshire
Printed in Great Britain by Bell and Bain Ltd, Glasgow

Contents

£15.00

Foreword v

Preface vii

Acknowledgements viii

Glossary ix

1. **Epilepsy Diagnosis, Classification and Treatment** 1
   Introduction
   Definitions of epilepsy
   Causes and classification of epilepsy seizures and
     syndromes
   Investigations
   What is a seizure?
   Epilepsies and epileptic syndromes
   Treatment
   Other treatments for epilepsy
   Epilepsy in adolescence
   Epilepsy and genetics

2. **Assessment** 22
   Educational and cognitive assessment
   Interpretation of assessment results
   The role of the educational psychologist
   Impact on the family
   First contact: the General Practitioner
   Experience of having tests
   Seeing the consultant
   What parents would have liked

3. **Implications for School, Classroom and Learning** 39
   What parents say they were told about the Code of
     Practice
   Sources of information for schools
   Who receives this information?
   Parents' comments about giving drugs
   Knowledge about the side effects of medication
   What happens after a seizure at school?
   Lack of understanding about the condition
   Lack of cooperation

Negative perceptions of school
Positive experiences of school

4. **Access to the Curriculum – A Whole-School Approach**   **58**
   Academic subjects
   Key Stage test and formal examination arrangements
   Examinations and assessed work
   Practical subjects and laboratory-based work
   Physical education, outdoor pursuits and swimming

5. **Epilepsy and Behaviour**   **68**
   Social aspects

6. **Language and Communication Problems Associated with Epilepsy and Related Syndromes**   **82**
   Epilepsy-related factors
   Types of seizures
   Medication effect
   Seizure frequency and duration
   Language and communication problems associated with epilepsy syndromes (or associated syndromes where epilepsy is a major feature)
   Management issues and principles
   General principles of management and support of children with language disability and epilepsy

7. **Quality of Life**   **95**
   Epilepsy surveys of quality of life
   Risk management
   Quality of life, learning disability and epilepsy

Useful Addresses/Internet Sites   105

Bibliography   110

Index   116

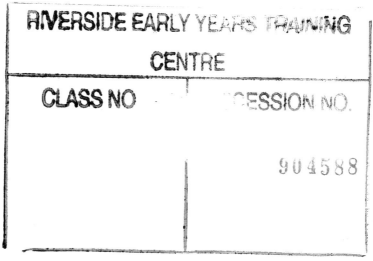
RIVERSIDE EARLY YEARS TRAINING CENTRE

CLASS NO	CESSION NO.
	904588

Foreword

Epilepsy is a condition which historically carried an 'aura' of mystery and fear. The image of possession in folk lore, literature and religion led to much of the stigmatisation in western societies through the centuries. But modern education has no place for damaging, irrational fears on the part of its practitioners. The life chances of our students in all spheres of education are heavily dependent upon the academic and social environment of educational institutions.

Whether symptoms of epilepsy are the secondary results of some diagnosed organic origin or whether they are 'idiopathic', without any clearly evident cause, they should not bar any of our young people from achieving their maximum potential. Whereas some pupils will bear significant medical syndromes, with damaging results upon their attainments, we should avoid leaping to pathological explanations or excuses for widespread limited performance. The lawyers, media figures, artists, schoolteachers, academics, nurses, doctors (including consultant physicians) and international sports people who have epilepsy are certainly an under-representation of those who could be making more of their lives.

The average primary school of 400 pupils will probably have around three pupils with epilepsy, whereas a large secondary school with 1,500 pupils may have ten. This book will be an advance in providing knowledge for a wide range of teachers, parents and other professionals involved with children and young people who have epilepsy. It includes evidence-based concerns of students with epilepsy, and will be particularly useful for parents and for carers. As much of the content is rooted in the centrality of young people's own experiences and needs, rather than in the sometimes excessive stress on their medical condition, many of those people who need information for their day-to-day practice in teaching, assessing and supporting their pupils will be helped by its contents. With its extensive bibliography it will also help those who want to engage in more advanced study of the subject in relation to special educational needs and enhanced quality of life.

Perhaps the thought that should be in the minds of those

who still need to address their stereotypical image of epilepsy should be the realisation that epilepsy is not a mystery. Indeed, the mystery is not why some people develop epilepsy in their lives, so much as why many of us do not.

> ... he [Caesar] hath the falling-sickness.

> No, Caesar hath it not; but you, and I,
> And honest Casca, we have the falling-sickness.

Julius Caesar, Act 1, Sc. 2.

Mike Harnor
Trustee and Member of the Council of Management,
British Epilepsy Association

Preface

This book is aimed at a wide audience. This is inevitable, as epilepsy and its treatment touches every aspect of life for those who are affected by it. The two authors work in very different settings and therefore have different styles of writing. We see this as one of the book's strengths. Each style is appropriate to the subject matter being considered.

The book owes much to the foresight and generosity of the British Epilepsy Association (BEA) who commissioned the Manchester Metropolitan University to investigate the effects of the Code of Practice for the Assessment and Identification of Pupils with SEN on children with epilepsy. It quickly became clear to the researchers that the families wanted to talk about much more than that and so, with additional funds from the BEA, the project developed into a major study of the experience of the assessment and treatment of epilepsy.

Some readers will notice that we do not refer in any detail to those who also have Autistic Spectrum Disorder (ASD). It has been suggested to us that this is an omission, as some writers have identified a significant co-morbidity. However, our publisher already has one book dealing with Autism and another with Asperger Syndrome. Those interested in the area may refer to these. We also feel that ASD is too large a subject to treat even in a full chapter and so, on both counts, a conscious decision was taken to leave it out.

Further, this is not a book from which people may seek detailed information on medical diagnoses or to ascertain the use and potential effects of anti-epileptic drugs. This subject is covered much more fully in other works specifically aimed at professions allied to medicine. Nevertheless, we do commend this practical guide to all those individuals involved and/or interested in epilepsy in children and young people, be they parents, carers or professionals. As authors with an active interest in the subject, we both felt strongly that it was timely to offer accurate information in an accessible and user-friendly style on a topic relevant to many thousands of people.

We hope you enjoy reading it as much as we have enjoyed collaborating on it.

Acknowledgements

The authors would like to express their heartfelt thanks to the following friends and colleagues who helped to translate this book from an idea to reality. Without their knowledgeable views and advice we should not have been able to write it.

Dr Juliet Goldbart, Reader in the Department of Psychology and Speech Pathology, Manchester Metropolitan University;

Dr Rosemary Newton, Associate Specialist in Childhood Epilepsy and Manager of Children's Assessment Service, David Lewis Centre, Alderley Edge, Cheshire;

Professor Peter Farrell, Research and Graduate Dean, Educational Support and Inclusion Research and Teaching Group, School of Education, University of Manchester;

British Epilepsy Association and the families who participated in a survey for the BEA;

Liz Thomas, Research Assistant at Manchester Metropolitan University;

Mike Harnor, Senior Lecturer, Department of Applied Community Studies, Manchester Metropolitan University; and

All the children who have attended the Children's Epilepsy Assessment Unit and school at the David Lewis Centre in Cheshire over the past few years.

Glossary

absence seizures: a generalised seizure (formerly called petit mal). Consciousness is altered briefly and it can appear that a person is daydreaming or is suffering a lapse in concentration or attention. Such episodes can occur frequently in a day and may significantly impair an individual's ability to follow conversation and absorb complex information. It is characterised by a specific three per second spike and wave pattern on an EEG. Absences are usually easily treated and many forms will disappear in adolescence. Note: other types of seizure can sometimes look like absences.

aetiology or etiology: the cause of the epilepsy.

ambulatory EEG: an EEG of the brain during normal activities. It is obtained by connecting very small electrodes to a portable recorder, like a 'Walkman'.

anatomical: relating to a part of the body's structure.

automatism: complex or purposeless movements that accompany or are associated with complex partial seizures e.g. lip smacking, chewing, clothes plucking, swallowing, humming.

brain haemorrhages: see **stroke**.

chronic: long lasting.

complex-partial seizures: a seizure involving one part of the brain where the level of consciousness or awareness of surroundings is impaired.

consultant: a doctor or surgeon who has received advanced specialised training in one field of medicine.

cryptogenic: an epilepsy that has an origin or cause of unknown or obscure origin, which has not been found.

CT (computerised tomography) scan: known as a CAT scan, a method of examining parts of complicated structures such as the brain using small doses of X-rays combined with advanced computer analysis.

diabetes mellitus: often just called 'diabetes', this is a disorder of the pancreas causing a deficiency of insulin. It results in excessive thirst and excretion of abnormally large quantities of urine containing an excess of glucose (sugar).

diagnosis: determining the cause of an illness or condition.

electrocardiogram (ECG): a recording of the electric currents produced by the beating heart, obtained by placing electrodes on the chest. It is used to diagnose possible heart disorders.

electroencephalogram (EEG): a tracing of the electrical activity that comes from the brain obtained by placing electrodes on the scalp. These may be connected to a pen recorder, but increasingly a computer is more likely to be used for interpretation by a specialist physician. It helps to diagnose the type and origin of a seizure and gives information on the amount of electrical activity produced between seizures (inter-ictally).

encephalitis: infection of the brain caused by bacterial or viral infection, resulting in inflammation.

epilepsy specialist nurse: a nurse who has received special training to enable her/him to support people with epilepsy. Many are initially established as Sapphire nurses, funded by the British Epilepsy Association under agreed conditions with the hospital trust or local primary care group.

epileptic focus: a local area of the brain which may be abnormal and can cause spike or certain wave patterns on an EEG.

epileptiform: characteristic of epilepsy (may refer to EEG pattern).

episodic: seizures which happen occasionally or sporadically.

febrile seizures: a seizure associated with a high temperature. These usually affect babies and young children under five years of age and are caused by the increased susceptibility of the young brain to seizures. Only rarely associated with later onset of epilepsy in older children.

focal seizures: see **partial seizures**.

frontal lobe epilepsy (fle): can be difficult to diagnose because of its links with other parts of the brain e.g. the temporal lobes. Complex partial seizures are common in this type of epilepsy, often occuring at night. These are often short and tend to happen in clusters. The child may have associated short repetitive movements e.g. cycling, stepping, kicking. Behaviour can appear over excited or bizzare. The child may call out unexpectedly. In other seizures muscle jerking may predominate.

generalised epilepsy: epileptic seizures which involve all of the brain. Tonic, clonic, atonic and absence seizures are all generalised in type.

idiopathic: also called 'familial', an epilepsy for which no cause can be found but which may have a family history.

infantile spasms (also known as West syndrome): a special form of epilepsy commencing in the first year of life. Causes are various. The spasms often appear as a series of between 5 and 50 a day and are characterised by sudden head jerks forward onto the chest, knees drawing up (without the discomfort shown in colic) and arms thrown outward in an extended way.

insulin: a hormone secreted by the pancreas that controls the concentration of glucose in the blood. Lack of it causes diabetes mellitus.

intelligence quotient (IQ): a number denoting the ratio of a person's intelligence to the statistical norm, 100 being average. In an IQ test, different brain functions are analysed by neuropsychological testing to show how well a person can solve problems, understand language, perceive and organise tasks of various kinds.

inter-ictal: the period between one seizure and the next.

local seizures: see **partial seizures**.

magnetic resonance imaging (MRI): a similar procedure to the CAT scan using magnetic fields rather than X-rays to create images of brain structure and density. Provides more detailed pictures than CT.

meningitis: infection of the membranes that surround the brain or spinal cord. This causes inflammation that if not treated promptly can result in brain damage or even death.

myoclonus (myoclonic seizure): sudden jerks or jolting of an arm, leg, shoulder or other part of the body involving a muscle group. Most people experience such occasional jerks before the onset of sleep. Repeated jerks in the form of seizures are found in some hard-to-treat epilepsy syndromes.

neuron or neurone: also called a nerve cell, a cell that conducts nerve impulses consisting of a cell body, axon and dendrites.

partial seizures: seizures that only involve part of the brain. May be associated with either improved or retained level of consciousness. They may be brief and subtle or involve complex movements outside of the person's control.

petit mal: see **absence seizures**.

photosensitive epilepsy: seizures caused by flickering and/or very bright lights. Sometimes known as a type of reflex epilepsy they can result in the person being afraid to watch television, use a computer or go to a disco.

post-ictal (post-seizure): refers to the period of time just after a seizure.

post-natal: occurring after birth.

pre-ictal (pre-seizure): refers to the period of time just before a seizure.

repetitive or prolonged seizures: also called status epilepticus, a situation in which the person has a long seizure or a second seizure before regaining consciousness from the first. This can be life threatening if not dealt with promptly. May become a medical emergency.

seizure: name for an epileptic event that involves a sudden, excessive electrical discharge affecting the transmission of messages in the brain. This results in altered brain function or behaviour in the part of the brain affected by the activity.

stroke: formerly called apoplexy, this is the bursting of a blood vessel in the brain. It results in loss of consciousness because the blood supply (and therefore oxygen) to part of the brain is reduced and usually causes damage (mild or severe) to the affected part. It can also result in loss of movement, speech and/or language and other brain functions.

symptomatic epilepsy: a type or group of epilepsies in which the underlying cause is known.

syndromal diagnosis: a diagnosis made as a result of careful mapping of the person's symptoms, which form a characteristic 'pattern' or 'profile'.

temporal lobe epilepsy (TLE): involves seizures starting in the part of the brain known as the temporal lobe. It may respond well to anti-convulsant drug (AED) treatment and may also be improved with surgery. About 60 per cent of complex partial seizures start in the temporal lobe. Can cause problems with temporary speech arrest during a seizure. Also associated with certain types of language problems. Post-ictal (post-seizure) confusion and dysphasia common. Can have associated motor and perceptual difficulties – usually temporary.

tertiary level: treatment in a hospital or unit in a hospital specialising in the treatment of one condition or offering a very high standard of a treatment in a specialist area of interest.

tonic-clonic seizure: a type of generalised seizure affecting the whole brain and characterised by stiffening of limbs followed by rhythmical jerking. This may last from seconds up to several minutes.

tumour: a mass of tissue formed by an uncontrolled growth of cells. This growth can be either **benign**, i.e. not threatening to life or health or **malignant**, i.e. uncontrollable, rapid-spreading and possibly fatal.

vagal nerve stimulators (VNS): rather like pacemakers, they stimulate a nerve (the vagus) involved in sending and receiving messages from the brain. This is thought to inhibit the onset of seizures.

video-EEG: a video camera used in conjunction with an EEG to record the onset and particular characteristics or features of seizures or similar episodes while being monitored simultaneously on an (ambulatory) EEG. It helps to diagnose seizures and the areas of the brain where there is a potential problem.

Chapter 1

Epilepsy Diagnosis, Classification and Treatment

Introduction

Epilepsy in children can be the result of problems in the central nervous system (the brain and associated organs which send and receive messages from it). Information on epilepsy can be found in medical textbooks on neurological conditions in childhood and adolescence. However, with the exception of a few journal articles and an early book by Rogan (1992), there is very little accessible, practically oriented material available to help people involved in the care and education of this group of children.

This book aims to fill this gap. It discusses epilepsy, its management and its impact on the quality of life of both the children and the people involved in their daily lives.

Definitions of epilepsy

Epilepsy is more common than is generally imagined. It occurs more frequently than diabetes and is the second most common neurological condition after migraine (Hopkins and Appleton 1996). Unlike diabetes it is not an illness or a disease but a symptom of an underlying problem with the functioning of a child's brain.

One of the earliest scientific definitions of epilepsy in neurophysiological terms was that by Jackson (1873) cited in *Braine's Diseases of the Nervous System* (Walton 1985) as being the 'name for sudden excessive rapid and local discharges of grey matter'.

Although this was accepted as the definitive description of epilepsy for many years, with our increased knowledge of the way the cells in the brain transmit and receive electrical messages we can do better. The word epilepsy is derived from a Greek word meaning 'to take hold of' – hence the use of the term 'seizure' to describe its effects. Epilepsy can also be described as a tendency to have repeated seizures. The seizures are an outward, visible sign that a part of the brain is not working as it should. Its activity of transmitting and receiving electrical and chemical messages becomes disrupted. The neurones (nerve cells) that carry the messages send them in a different order, or too strongly (as excessive electrical discharges), which can result in the person having a seizure. The way in which a seizure affects what someone says, does or feels depends on the location of the problem in the brain and how far the disruption spreads. A seizure can start by affecting one part of the brain, then spread to affect another part, or even the whole brain. This is why people can experience different types of seizures lasting from a few seconds to several minutes.

There are many types of epilepsy and seizures. Lists have been supplied by the International League Against Epilepsy (ILAE) (Commission on Classification and Terminology of the International League Against Epilepsy 1981, 1985, 1989) and Engel (2001) has tried to produce a complete list. We will deal later with why it is important to know the epilepsy and seizure categories.

About 35 new cases of a focal epilepsy syndrome (see 1.1 and 1.3) will be diagnosed each year for every million people in the population (Oxbury *et al*. 2000). Sadly, 15 to 20 of these people cannot be helped even by modern drug therapy. The British Epilepsy Association (BEA) estimates that at any one time, 1 in 150 people in the UK will have epilepsy. However, the incidence and variation in seizure frequency and type is at its greatest in children. Oxbury *et al*. stress how 'maturational factors are potent modifiers of early epileptic phenomena, influencing both partial and generalised disorders', especially in the first ten years of life (children will tend to grow out of it). Appleton and Gibbs (1998) stated that (at the time of going to press) there were no precise data available on the prevalence of epilepsy in children. They quote 0.7–0.8 per cent of all school children in the UK aged 5–17 years as the figure most often mentioned in the research literature. Based on the Office of Population Censuses and Surveys data (1991), Appleton and Gibbs estimated that at any one time in England, Scotland and Wales there would be approximately 61,000 children with active epilepsy. Although these figures may appear startling, approximately one-third of all epilepsies that begin in childhood will have apparently disappeared by the onset of adolescence.

Epilepsy can be caused or 'provoked' in a number of ways, e.g. by an accident or head injury (although a head injury does not always cause epilepsy). Epilepsy is categorised along two axes, 'anatomical' and 'aetiological', depending on whether the cause is known or only suspected. The aetiological classifications (see Table 1.1) are grouped according to familial (idiopathic), symptomatic (identified underlying cause) or cryptogenic (where an underlying cause is suspected but has not been identified), (see later).

A child is more likely to develop epilepsy if an accident or head injury was followed by a long period of unconsciousness or bleeding in the brain. The type of seizure they might experience will depend on the part of the brain that has been damaged.

Epilepsy can be caused by infections of the brain – including meningitis and encephalitis, or infections causing abscesses to develop in the brain – as well as tumours of all kinds, either benign or malignant (see Fig. 1.1). Sometimes epilepsy can develop because the brain was not properly developed prior to birth, the cells were not 'laid down' in the correct order, or there was an imbalance of the different types of cell required for correct functioning of the brain. Occasionally a difficult birth

Causes and classification of epilepsy seizures and syndromes

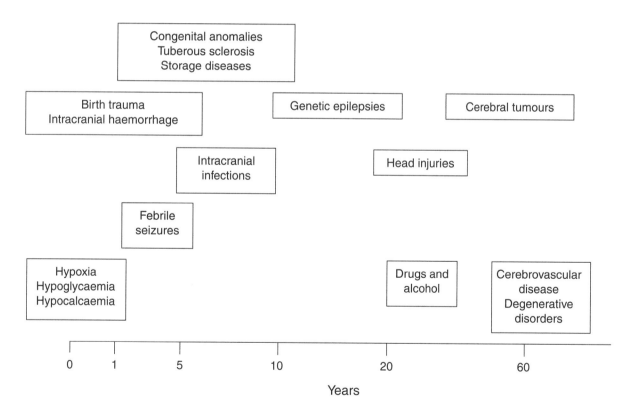

Figure 1.1 Causes of seizures and epilepsy by age
(Reproduced from D. Chadwick, N. Cartlidge and D. Bates (eds) (1989) *Medical Neurology*. Edinburgh: Churchill-Livingstone.)

• **Symptomatic**	where a known cause is found, e.g. head injury, CNS infection (e.g. bacterial meningitis, tumours, structural abnormalities or metabolic disorders)
• **Cryptogenic**	where no cause is found but an underlying abnormality is suspected
• **Idiopathic**	no cause is found but a genetic causal link is suspected

Table 1.1

during which the baby is deprived of oxygen can cause brain damage, leading later to epilepsy. Sometimes oxygen deprivation can also occur during pregnancy, leading to problems after the baby is born.

No specific cause can be found for cryptogenic epilepsies, although one might be suspected. Even though such diagnostic investigations as magnetic resonance imaging (MRI) scans have improved immeasurably in recent years, tests are still not always elaborate or detailed enough to pinpoint precisely the cause of the problem in a child's brain (see Table 1.1).

Idiopathic epilepsies have no clear underlying cause. However, children with this type of epilepsy generally have a strong family history of epilepsy suggesting a genetic factor (genetics and epilepsy are discussed in more detail later in this chapter). See Table 1.2 for information on diagnosis.

Investigations

When doctors explain how to diagnose epilepsy, the most important thing they emphasise (and often the least recognised or acknowledged), is the child's medical history. Within that, the most important information is a detailed description (or descriptions if they are different) of the 'episodes' under

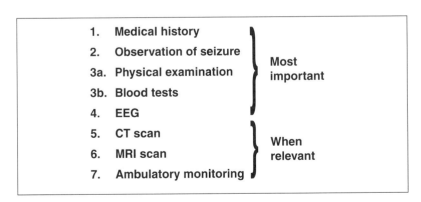

Table 1.2

investigation. If the child lost consciousness during the episode, or cannot remember clearly the order and details of the event, then it is helpful if anyone who witnessed it either writes an account of what they saw, or accompanies the parents to visit the doctor. Results from tests and other investigations (listed in Table 1.2) will confirm, support or question a diagnosis, but ultimately it will be the seizure description that should provide evidence of epilepsy. It will also contribute to a classification of an epilepsy syndrome. Additional tests will help to determine the cause of the episode or series of episodes ('seizure events'). Sometimes, for instance, the child may need to have blood tests to eliminate problems caused by the liver, heart or kidneys. An electrocardiogram (ECG) may need to be taken to check that the child's heart is working properly. People may faint or have a seizure for a variety of reasons, but this does not automatically mean that they have epilepsy. It may take a number of seemingly irrelevant tests and a long time before a diagnosis can be made.

It is quite probable that the individual concerned will have an electroencephalogram (EEG). This is a machine that measures electrical impulses in the brain as its neuro-transmitters (message senders and receivers) communicate with one another. About 20 per cent of people with epilepsy will have a normal EEG; others will have an 'inconclusive result' unless they actually experience a seizure while their brainwaves are being recorded. One way of overcoming the problem of seizure capture is for the child or young person to wear an EEG monitor (called an ambulatory EEG) for several days. However, it should be noted that many people may have 'discharges' or 'abnormalities' in their EEG recordings and yet do not have either symptoms of epilepsy or anything else significantly wrong with their brains.

An ambulatory EEG is like a portable cassette player with wires (leads) attached to about eight electrodes that are glued to the scalp. Tapes or discs record the electrical impulses in the brain and are changed every few hours until the testing has finished. This kind of monitoring is useful if the effects of behaviours, mood swings, and changes in levels of concentration or exposure to stressful situations need to be checked. The child may take psychological tests or do school work while attached to the EEG, with simultaneous video recording being carried out. In this way more subtle seizures such as absences, which have a distinctive tracing on an EEG recording, can be mapped both visually and electronically. The doctor can also determine from which part of the brain a seizure starts, how and where its effect spreads, its duration and how quickly the brain recovers afterwards. EEG recordings can also help to pinpoint certain epilepsy syndromes as they provide a classic 'signature' associated with each type. One syndrome for example, called 'continuous spike-waves during slow-wave sleep' (CSWS or ESES, see later) only displays such abnormal EEG patterns when the child is very drowsy or completely asleep. Another distinctive EEG pattern is associated with primary generalised epilepsy, one of the more common epilepsies of childhood, in which seizures usually occur within a couple of hours of waking.

Normally our brains create electrical waves that occur about ten times a second. If the EEG shows spikes or spike/wave patterns, there is a significant possibility that the child may have epilepsy.

If the evidence is still inconclusive, or the doctor wants to find out more about the cause and possible treatment options available, she/he may choose to refer the child or young person for a CT scan (computerised tomography or CAT scan). 'Slices' of the brain are scanned to determine if there are any tumours present or damage caused by strokes or other brain haemorrhages. Occasionally dye may be injected into a vein in the arm to see what is happening in parts of the brain's structure. This involves the child lying still for several minutes. Although it doesn't hurt, some children find it difficult to lie still and they may be given a mild sedative to help them relax.

CT technology is now being superseded by MRI, which is able to pick up more subtle changes in size and density of brain structures. It can locate small scars and lesions in the brain, previously undetectable by CT. MRI is assuming increasing importance as one of the ways in which doctors may be helped to decide whether surgery might be useful for epilepsy in adults and children. However, not all children will need to have either an MRI or CT scan; the former only tends to be used when a structural abnormality is suspected.

Despite the advances in technology and increased knowledge of the brain and its functions, about 70 per cent of people with epilepsy will not know the cause of the problem in their brain which provokes a seizure. Some epilepsies are caused by head injury or infections in childhood, but as previously mentioned, others may be the result of abnormal development of the brain in the foetus before birth. Genetic factors may also have played a role. In all cases, as technology advances we are gaining a greater understanding of the causes and treatments for this complex condition. Sometimes the cause can be treated, but for some children the emphasis lies in controlling and managing their seizures and ensuring they achieve the best possible quality of life.

What is an epileptic seizure? It is important to know this because teachers and others may not only see a child having one, but also be asked subsequently to describe it. An example of a seizure description form is provided in Figure 1.3. However, it is helpful to appreciate from the outset both what to look for in your observation of the child having a seizure (or fit), and what to expect. Most people have never witnessed a seizure and the fear is generally far worse than actually being present when an 'event' happens. It is reassuring to know what to expect and how to react since there are still many misconceptions about what a bystander should do (see pp. 15 and 16).

If a child in your class, care or with whom you are working has epilepsy, then you should find out:

- the type of seizures the child experiences;
- their frequency and whether they occur nocturnally (at night) or at specific times of the day, week or month;
- any potential trigger factors, e.g. watching a film, certain types of lighting, hunger, fatigue, changes in activity;
- how the seizure should be dealt with should it occur (see pp. 15 and 16).

Only a brief description of the main seizure types is provided here. You are recommended to read the excellent book, *Epilepsy in Childhood and Adolescence* (Appleton and Gibbs 1998) for more detailed descriptions, medical background and management issues.

Seizures may be divided into two broad categories, partial (local or focal) and generalised. As the names imply, the former

What is a seizure?

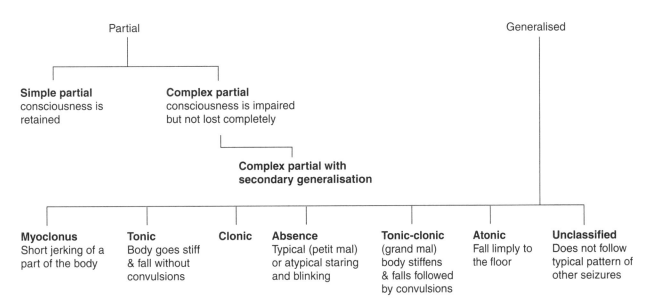

Figure 1.2 Classification of seizure types between partial and generalised

affects only one lobe or part of one side of the brain whereas the latter affects the whole brain. Sometimes a seizure can start as localised and then in a matter of seconds generalise to affect the entire brain (see Figure 1.2).

Partial seizures may be further subdivided according to the part of the brain affected and the symptoms associated with it.

Thus it is possible to have simple partial seizures with:

- motor symptoms, e.g. a trembling hand;
- somatosensory or special sensory symptoms, e.g. butterflies in stomach or experiencing an odd smell;
- autonomic symptoms, e.g. lip smacking; or
- psychic symptoms, e.g. a hallucination.

Epilepsies and epileptic syndromes

Assigning a child's epilepsy to an epilepsy syndrome may help to select the best type of treatment, give some idea of the prognosis (i.e. what to expect in the future) and help to establish what might have caused the epilepsy. A diagnosis aids parents, teachers and professionals to understand some of the problems a child might experience during their course of development, learning, language and cognition. In some instances, a child may acquire some skills and then lose them, or they might experience problems with attention, short-term memory or with reading and writing. Therefore it is important to establish a syndromic diagnosis in the 60 per cent or so of the cases where this can be achieved.

Epilepsies and epileptic syndromes are classified in two ways:

a) anatomical, e.g. localisation-related or generalised and
b) according to the epilepsy's aetiology (see p. 4 and Table 1.3), e.g. symptomatic, cryptogenic or idiopathic.

For example, a child might be described as having symptomatic localisation-related epilepsy. Additionally, there is a third category of epilepsies where it is clinically impossible to determine whether the epilepsy is localisation related or generalised, plus a fourth category of 'special' or more unusual syndromes, which tend to occur in particular circumstances such as very high temperature or at certain ages as in febrile seizures (see Table 1.3).

The media in recent times has highlighted epilepsies that may be triggered by particular stimuli such as certain types of lighting or the flicker on computer and TV screens. This group of epilepsies are termed reflex epilepsies. Once a child has had

1. **Localisation-related (focal, local, partial) epilepsies and syndromes**
1.1 Idiopathic (with age-related onset)
   - benign childhood epilepsy with centro-temporal spikes
   - childhood epilepsy with occipital paroxysms
   - primary reading epilepsy
1.2 Symptomatic
   - chronic progressive epilepsia partialis continua of childhood (Kojewnikow's syndrome)*
   - syndromes characterised by seizures with specific modes of presentation
1.3 Cryptogenic (presumed symptomatic but aetiology unknown)

2. **Generalised epilepsies and syndromes**
2.1 Idiopathic (with age-related onset, listed in order of age)
   - benign neonatal familial convulsions
   - benign neonatal convulsions
   - benign myoclonic epilepsy in infancy
   - childhood absence epilepsy
   - juvenile absence epilepsy
   - juvenile myoclonic epilepsy
   - epilepsy with grand mal (generalised tonic-clonic seizures on awakening)
   - other generalised idiopathic epilepsies not defined above
   - epilepsies with seizures precipitated by specific modes of activation (reflex and reading epilepsies)
2.2 Cryptogenic or symptomatic (in order of age)
   - West's syndrome
   - Lennox-Gastaut syndrome
   - epilepsy with myoclonic-astatic seizures
   - epilepsy with myoclonic absences
2.3 Symptomatic
   2.3.1 Non-specific aetiology
      - early myoclonic encephalopathy
      - early infantile epileptic encephalopathy with suppression burst
      - other symptomatic generalised epilepsies not defined above
   2.3.2 Specific syndromes/aetiologies
      - cerebral malformations
      - inborn errors of metabolism including pyridoxine dependency and disorders frequently presenting as progressive myoclonic epilepsy

3. **Epilepsies and syndromes undetermined, whether focal or generalised**
3.1 With both generalised and focal seizures
   - neonatal seizures
   - severe myoclonic epilepsy in infancy
   - epilepsy with continuous spike-waves during slow-wave sleep (ESES)**
   - acquired epileptic aphasia (Landau-Kleffner syndrome)
   - other undetermined epilepsies not defined above
3.2 Without unequivocal generalised or focal features

4. **Special syndromes**
4.1 Situation-related seizures
   - febrile convulsions
   - isolated seizures or isolated status epilepticus
   - seizures occurring only when there is an acute metabolic or toxic event due to factors such as alcohol, drugs, eclampsia, non-ketotic hyperglycinaemia
   - reflex epilepsy

* more commonly known as Rasmussen's syndrome; ** now known as CSWS – see Chapter 6.

Table 1.3
(From Commission on Classification and Terminology of the International League Against Epilepsy, 'Proposal for classification of epilepsies and epileptic syndromes', *Epilepsia* (1989) **30**, 389–99.)

such an attack, the fear of it recurring can actually make its recurrence more likely. Such triggers may have a clear psychological component to them. Appleton and Gibbs (1998) list several potential trigger factors that can provoke a seizure in children with this diagnosis. Triggers include:

- flicker-, flash- or pattern-induced (photosensitive);
- reading;
- a startle reflex;
- eating-induced;
- immersion in hot or cold water;
- mathematic- or calculation-induced.

Photosensitive epilepsy is the most common. Given the right intensity, frequency and length of exposure a child will probably experience either a myoclonic jerk (rather like a jerk experienced when falling asleep) or a tonic-clonic seizure with consequent loss of consciousness that may last a few seconds or minutes. Often there is a family history of similar types of epilepsy, more frequently in girls than boys. They tend to occur most often, though not exclusively, in children and young people aged 10–18 years, fading as they reach their 20s. Photosensitive epilepsy is found only in younger children when they have symptomatic or cryptogenic epilepsy, i.e. when a cause for the condition is not known or only suspected.

Treatment

There are several forms of treatment for epilepsy and epileptic seizures. It is important for a number of reasons to find out what treatment the child or young person is currently receiving. The people responsible for the child need to know:

- whether special arrangements are necessary for pills to be taken during the school day;
- any arrangements for medical help which may be required if a seizure longer than normal is experienced, if breathing becomes impaired or if they do not recover from one seizure before going into another (a rare medical condition called status epilepticus);
- any side effects caused by the pills;
- changes in the treatment that might affect academic performance, participation in physical activities or increased susceptibility to seizures until the new medication regime settles down.

When changes have been made in seizure management, such as alterations to the amount, type and times of taking drugs, you may be asked to watch for any changes in the child or young person. Sometimes this can be difficult – especially as you may not always be sure what you are supposed to be watching for! However, your observations can help the doctors and nurses and other professionals involved in case management to make the correct, and importantly, informed decisions which will help to maintain or improve that individual's quality of life as well as academic performance.

What might you be asked to look for? This question will be returned to in later chapters of the book, but the information most frequently requested concerns witnessed seizures. You may never see a child having a seizure since, for example, they may only have them at night or on waking in the early morning. Nevertheless, as discussed earlier, seizures may be triggered or provoked by a variety of stimuli. There are several features concerning the lead-up to a seizure, how it presents and what follows, which provide useful evidence on which medical, social and educational management decisions can be made. One of the best and most efficient ways of recording such information in a logical and methodical manner is by using seizure record forms and charts (see Figures 1.3, 1.4 and 1.5).

What should you do if a child in your care has a seizure?

Read the following example of Jane, aged nine, described by a member of staff on playground duty. Jane has epilepsy, but has never been known to have a seizure at school.

> Jane is playing outside in the sunshine with her friends one morning. Her friend comes running up to the teacher on playground duty. 'Come quickly,' calls Jane's friend. 'Something has happened to Jane.' The teacher finds Jane at the edge of the hard play area making odd, gurgling and grunting sounds. Her arms and legs are jerking. Her face has lost all colour and she is sweating. Jane's teacher gently rolls her on one side and places a folded sweatshirt she has borrowed from another child under her head. She looks round to make sure Jane's arms and legs will not come into contact with any hard objects. She knows from the guidelines provided by the school, not to try to put anything in Jane's mouth, as it would do more harm than good. Gradually the seizure subsides. The teacher stays beside Jane. She realises that Jane will

need to sleep somewhere quietly after the seizure is over. At the very least Jane will need reassurance of where she is and that everything is all right. The teacher asks one of the other children to fetch another member of staff and a wheelchair to be brought out, so they can wheel Jane to a quieter, more private part of the school, to recover.

When this had been organised, the teacher filled in a Seizure Record Sheet. She was not certain what sort of seizure she had witnessed so she ticked the 'Unclassified' box on the record sheet. She carefully noted the length of time the seizure had lasted – four minutes. It had seemed an eternity at the time. Looking at Jane's school records she noted that although Jane did not need any rescue medication, her parents liked to be notified if an 'event' happened during the school day. Jane's father was grateful that her school had not felt the need to call the emergency services and had allowed her to sleep quietly in the medical room for an hour and then return to class. Although Jane was tired and had a headache on returning home, there was no seizure recurrence and she attended school as usual the following day.

You may have noticed several points regarding how to manage such an episode should it happen while someone with epilepsy is with you.

1. Stay calm – not always easy when other children are around, or when you are in a public place or in a swimming pool.
2. If the person is unconscious turn them on their side. If they are jerking head, arms and legs, place something soft under their head and ensure limbs are not caught on hard objects or furniture.
3. Never try to insert something into their mouth.
4. Note the time the seizure started and finished.
5. If the seizure seems longer than usual – say by two or more minutes – if breathing seems to be difficult, or if the child goes into another seizure before fully recovering consciousness from the first one, or if there is an apparent or suspected head injury, summon medical assistance quickly. Lack of oxygen for any length of time to the brain can alter the way its metabolism works, thus putting it at risk of damage should the situation continue untreated. **Let the emergency services know how long the child has been unconscious.**

Children's Seizure Description Form

Child's details	**Name** .... **DoB** .... **Place** .... **Date** .... **Witnesses** .... **Time** ....
Prodrome	Did anything make you think a seizure was due? (e.g. illness, pre-ictal behaviour etc.)
Immediate triggers or antecedents	What happened just before? (e.g. argument, tantrum, frustration, watching TV, fall etc.)
Course of seizure	What did you see happen *first*? (e.g. consciousness, tone and posture, jerking, side and body parts involved, repetitive movements, colour, speech, behaviour, mobility, incontinence, etc.
Treatment given and response	*(If drugs used give name, route and timing of administration and response)*
Post-ictal phase and recovery	How was the child after the seizure? (e.g. sleeping, confused, wandering, behaviour, balance, etc.) How long to full recovery?
Duration	How long did the seizure last?
Other comments	
Staff seizure classification	What sort of seizure do you think this is?
For doctor's use	

Figure 1.3 Children's seizure description form. Reproduced by permission of David Lewis Centre, Cheshire (2001).

Name: _____ **Month:** _____ **Year:** _____

TONIC-CLONIC (MOD TONIC-CLONIC)

	1	2	3	4	5	6	7	8	9	10	11	12	13	14	15	16	17	18	19	20	21	22	23	24	25	26	27	28	29	30	31
SLEEP																															
AWAKE																															

TONIC

	1	2	3	4	5	6	7	8	9	10	11	12	13	14	15	16	17	18	19	20	21	22	23	24	25	26	27	28	29	30	31
SLEEP																															
AWAKE																															

ATONIC

	1	2	3	4	5	6	7	8	9	10	11	12	13	14	15	16	17	18	19	20	21	22	23	24	25	26	27	28	29	30	31
SLEEP																															
AWAKE																															

MYOCLONIC

	1	2	3	4	5	6	7	8	9	10	11	12	13	14	15	16	17	18	19	20	21	22	23	24	25	26	27	28	29	30	31
SLEEP																															
AWAKE																															

ABSENCE

	1	2	3	4	5	6	7	8	9	10	11	12	13	14	15	16	17	18	19	20	21	22	23	24	25	26	27	28	29	30	31
SLEEP																															
AWAKE																															

COMPLEX PARTIAL

	1	2	3	4	5	6	7	8	9	10	11	12	13	14	15	16	17	18	19	20	21	22	23	24	25	26	27	28	29	30	31
SLEEP																															
AWAKE																															

SIMPLE PARTIAL (AURA)

	1	2	3	4	5	6	7	8	9	10	11	12	13	14	15	16	17	18	19	20	21	22	23	24	25	26	27	28	29	30	31
SLEEP																															
AWAKE																															

UNCLASSIFIED

	1	2	3	4	5	6	7	8	9	10	11	12	13	14	15	16	17	18	19	20	21	22	23	24	25	26	27	28	29	30	31
SLEEP																															
AWAKE																															

Notes on completing the charts
1. Enter the number of seizures each day in the correct part of the chart
2. Divide the seizures into whether they happened from sleep or while awake
3. Fill in a description form giving details of what happened during the seizure
4. If you are not sure how to classify a seizure enter it in the unclassified section

Figure 1.4 Seizure record sheet

ALTERNATIVE SEIZURE RECORD CHART USED IN AN EPILEPSY CLINIC

Month _____   Year _____   Name _____

Date	1	2	3	4	5	6	7	8	9	10	11	12	13	14	15
Menstrual cycle															
Type of seizure	Indicate **M** = Myoclonic Jerks, **A** = Atonic Attacks, **T/C** = Tonic/Clonic Seizures, **C** = Clonic, **AB** = Absences, **R** = Reflex														
1															
2															
3															
4															
Duration of seizure															
1															
2															
3															
4															
Medication	Indicate name and amount reduced or increased														
PRN – Rescue Meds															

Date	16	17	18	19	20	21	22	23	24	25	26	27	28	29	30
Menstrual cycle															
Type of seizure	Indicate **M** = Myoclonic Jerks, **A** = Atonic Attacks, **T/C** = Tonic/Clonic Seizures, **C** = Clonic, **AB** = Absences, **R** = Reflex														
1															
2															
3															
4															
Duration of seizure															
1															
2															
3															
4															
Medication	Indicate name and amount reduced or increased														
PRN – Rescue Meds															

Figure 1.5   Monitoring of seizures. Reproduced by permission of CARE Project in association with the David Lewis Centre, Cheshire.

When someone has had a seizure and is starting to come round, others should be discouraged from gathering round the person. If possible, cover them with a rug or blanket as they will be embarrassed if they have been incontinent during their seizure. As soon as possible seek help to move them to a more appropriate location and clear any mess away as soon as you can.

6. Make sure that either you or someone they recognise stays with them to reassure them when they regain consciousness. At first, they are likely to be quite disoriented and unaware of what has happened.
7. Do not give them any food or drink until they have fully come round.
8. As soon as possible after the event make a note of what happened:
   a) just before the seizure occurred;
   b) during the seizure;
   c) immediately after, including how long it took for the child/person to recover (see Figures 1.3, 1.4 and 1.5).

Not all seizures are of the dramatic variety displayed on TV with convulsing legs and arms; they can be much more subtle. All books on epilepsy provide detailed descriptions of how seizures can be differentiated. There are also some excellent commercial videos available aimed at training staff groups, teachers, parents, nurses etc. (A list is available from the BEA and can be purchased via their website, see Useful Addresses/ Internet Sites.)

Other treatments for epilepsy

There are a number of alternative treatment options becoming increasingly available as knowledge about the brain, its chemical composition and functioning continues to develop and improve. The most well-known alternative to medication treatment is surgery. However, the child's epilepsy must accord with very specific criteria before surgery is considered a viable option. In particular, there needs to be clear and unambiguous evidence that seizures arise from a localised or focal area of the brain which is accessible and that surgery will not damage that person functionally in any way once the affected part of the brain has been removed.

Professionals involved with the care, support and teaching of children under consideration for an epilepsy surgery programme are often asked to provide evidence of current academic, cognitive, linguistic and other skills performance.

Such evidence, combined with other tests, will help the surgical team, together with the child and their parents, decide whether the benefits outweigh the risks of proceeding with such an operation, e.g. if the focus of the epilepsy is too close to the language area of the brain.

Vagal nerve stimulators (VNS) (rather like pacemakers) have been used in small-scale studies of children. The principle, as the name indicates, is to stimulate a nerve (the vagus) involved in sending and receiving messages to and from the brain. Although the underlying mechanism is uncertain, it is thought that the stimulation inhibits the onset of seizures. However, there is still much more research to be done in this area before definite conclusions can be drawn about its efficacy in children. Of interest here is that hoarseness and sometimes coughing were noted side effects in some VNS patients (Appleton and Gibbs 1998). As they intimate, it remains to be established exactly which children and which types of epileptic seizure and syndromes would benefit from this form of treatment regime.

Other therapies and treatments include:

- ketogenic (very high fat) low carbohydrate diet;
- steroid therapy;
- behavioural therapies;
- aromatherapy;
- acupuncture;
- herbal and homeopathic treatments.

For more detailed information, see the key epilepsy texts listed in the Bibliography or investigate one of the major epilepsy association websites (see Useful Addresses/Internet Sites).

Epilepsy in adolescence

The topic concerning issues relating specifically to epilepsy in adolescence will be returned to in the chapters relating to family issues, education and quality of life. However, there are a few points worthy of mention here.

Appleton and Gibbs (1998) quote figures of 75 teenagers per 100,000 having their first seizure in adolescence, with prevalence rates of 6–7 per 1,000. Some epilepsies, such as symptomatic partial epilepsy, are recognised as having onset after puberty, as are some of the idiopathic generalised epilepsies (Janz and Waltz 1994). Causes are not dissimilar to those found in younger children, although tumours are thought to be more common and of course there is the risk from substance and alcohol abuse.

In this group of young people, you need to be aware that what may be witnessed or reported to you as a seizure may not be epilepsy, but related to another condition such as:

- migraine;
- syncope (fainting);
- panic attack;
- substance abuse (especially cocaine, ecstasy, heroin and 'smack');
- non-epileptic attack disorder (previously called pseudo seizures).

Investigations similar to those used for differential diagnosis of the epilepsies of childhood will be used to establish a clear, differential diagnosis of the seizure and syndrome type. Other professionals, teachers and parents may be asked to provide information on the following in order to help make the diagnosis:

- any pre-disposing or antecedent factors that might precipitate a seizure;
- any family history of epilepsy;
- incidence and frequency of headaches;
- deterioration in academic performance;
- personality changes beyond those normally associated with the onset of puberty;
- any increase in attention and concentration difficulties;
- changes in behaviour and mood that appear out of the ordinary;
- suspicion of drug or alcohol abuse;
- a more erratic lifestyle felt to be out of character with previous behaviour.

Principles of treatment are similar to those for children, although management in secondary school and further education or higher education settings is slightly different in view of the older age group and more complex environments. Psychological support of teenagers with epilepsy is as important as physical and medical support. This can be overlooked by service providers, although some specialist epilepsy clinics and hospital out-patient services are addressing this issue in an effort to increase medication compliance and decrease the incidence of emergency admissions due to epilepsy-related problems. It is becoming increasingly recognised that this group of young people may require support from clinical, psychological and possibly psychiatric services, as well as neurology or specialist epilepsy (Sapphire) nurse practitioners.

The psychological, social and educational impacts of epilepsy will be discussed in subsequent chapters. However, it is the responsibility of us all to remain informed, to liaise and exchange information with relevant colleagues and parents, and to ensure the child or young person remains central in our efforts to provide support through the stages of assessment, diagnosis, treatment and management.

Epilepsy and genetics

This is a complicated area of knowledge, study and ongoing research in which our understanding of the relationship between epilepsy and genetics has improved meteorically in the last ten years. It is a subject that needs to be included here because when we are talking about the causes of epilepsy, it is estimated that up to 40 per cent of childhood epilepsies may have a genetic component of some kind. This component can be as non-specific as a child having an inherent predisposition to epilepsy. This is probably due to the inheritance of a few pre-disposing genes perhaps interacting with environmental factors – any of which would be insufficient on their own to cause epilepsy. There is then a second group where a specific 'disease' trait or characteristic within a family can be more clearly identified, caused by a mutation in a single gene of large effect (e.g. as in Table 1.4).

Epilepsy genes fall into clear groups. They can cause:

- abnormal brain development;
- progressive neurological degeneration (rare);
- disturbance in the way the brain metabolises energy; or
- a disturbance in the chemical transmission and electrical excitability in the brain.

Photosensitive epilepsy is also thought to have a genetic link in some instances. Twice as common in girls as boys, it occurs between the ages of ten and 16 and usually resolves itself by the end of adolescence.

Just because a child has a history of *febrile convulsions* associated with illness or a high temperature this does not necessarily imply that they will go on to develop epilepsy. *Childhood absence epilepsy (CAE)* is an idiopathic generalised epilepsy syndrome in which absences usually start when the child is between two and 12 years old. This syndrome, although clearly shown by family studies to be of genetic origin, is not due to a single gene defect but has complex inheritance. One of the susceptibility genes is on chromosome 8q24.

Juvenile Myoclonic Epilepsy (JME) is another idiopathic generalised epilepsy with complex inheritance, there is some evidence from a gene on chromosome 6p and same for a gene on chromosome 15. At present the details are not clear.

Benign Neonatal Febrile Convulsions (BNFC) is a rare epilepsy in babies but has a single (mendelian or single gene autosomal dominant) inheritance. It is now known to be carried by mutations in brain potassium channels (KCNQ2 or KCNQ3).

Generalised Epilepsy with Febrile Seizures Plus (GEFS+) is a recently described syndrome producing frontal epilepsy: different family members can have different seizures ranging from benigh febrile convulsions to myoclonic absence epilepsy to severe myoclonic epilepsy of infancy. It is now known to be caused by mutations in a brain sodium channel (e.g. SCNIB).

As mentioned earlier, the idiopathic group of epilepsies are those that it is presumed do not have associated metabolic or structural abnormalities and are therefore thought to have a genetic basis to their existence. Some are known to have an autosomal dominant link, some a recessive link, and some are too complex for this to be stated with any certainty at present.

Epilepsy can occur in a number of diseases and syndromes that are known to have single (mendelian) gene mutations. The most common ones are set out in Table 1.4.

However, much work still needs to be done in classifying the epilepsies with more than one gene involved (complex inheritance). More research will hopefully lead to a greater understanding of the causes of the epilepsies and the influence of environmental factors. Then, maybe such information can be used to provide improved management, genetic counselling and prevention of the more difficult-to-treat epilepsies whether rare single gene disorders such as Angelman's syndrome and tuberous sclerosis or common with complex inheritance such as JME and CAE.

DISORDER	INHERITANCE	OTHER NOTES
Tuberous sclerosis	Autosomal dominant – two different genetic loci 9q and 16q	Neurocutaneous syndrome Types of epilepsy tend to be age related Epilepsy in 80% Learning disability in 50%
Fragile X syndrome	X-linked	Epilepsy occurs in 20–40% All seizure types Develops early and remits in adolescence. Responds well to anti-convulsant treatment
Angelman's syndrome	Carried on maternal chromosome	Epilepsy develops in 90% and is resistant to treatment in at least 50%. All seizures are common seizures and not problematic in adulthood
Rett syndrome	X-linked (thought to be dominant)	Seizures occur in 70–80%, usually first noticed between 3 and 5 years. Some behavioural abnormalities can be mistaken for seizures. Becomes less troublesome in adulthood
Neurofibromatosis Types 1 and 2	Autosomal dominant	Neurocutaneous syndrome
Huntington's disease	Autosomal dominant	Epilepsy with other manifestations
Down's syndrome	Trisomy 21	Seizures in less than10% but nearly 50% of those have onset in first year of life. All seizure types but tonic-clonic are most common

Table 1.4

Chapter 2

Assessment

Educational and cognitive assessment

This chapter looks at assessment and its impact on the child and the family. We will examine precisely what is being assessed and why. We will look at assessing in special circumstances and the role of professionals. In particular, we will examine the role of educational psychologists at local education authority (LEA) level, school level and at the level of the individual child.

Do we need to assess? The following examples show how important it is to make a thorough multi-disciplinary assessment of the non-medical aspects of a child's ability and performance and to continue monitoring on a regular basis.

> Melanie was four years old and had recently been given a diagnosis of epilepsy. She had attended pre-school nursery for three days a week for the last six months and her family were pleased that she had apparently settled into the pre-school nursery group so well. One day, just before the summer holidays, Melanie brought a letter home from her nursery teacher, Mrs Jones. Melanie's mother read the letter. It said, 'Melanie has been a bright and popular member of the nursery group in the time she has been with us. However, she has been struggling with the reading readiness work we have been doing with her and we wonder whether she could delay moving into Reception class until at least after Christmas, possibly longer. Could you and Melanie's father spare some time to come in for a meeting with her new Reception teacher to be, and we will ask our educational psychologist if she can join us too?' Melanie's mother wondered whether she should have mentioned Melanie's increase in night-time seizures to Mrs Jones. Maybe that was why Melanie was so tired and difficult to cope with in the mornings.
>
> Clearly, Melanie's mother and father need to meet Mrs Jones,

Melanie's future teacher, and the educational psychologist as soon as possible. Maybe there were other problems the nursery were not telling her about. Was Melanie struggling with her pre-number work too? And what was she like at concentrating when they did small group work or played games? Melanie's mother had noticed that Melanie had been becoming increasingly distractible of late but had put this down to her interrupted sleeping at night of late. Was Melanie behind in any of her other 'work'? Melanie's mother tried to remember what John and Martin, Melanie's brothers, had been doing when they transferred from nursery to Reception. It was difficult. It all happened a while ago and it was hard to recall who had done what at that age.

Is Melanie behaving differently from her peers? How can we be objective about our observations of her performance? Six or seven months' difference in age can make such a difference at this time in children's lives. Is one aspect of Melanie's learning more problematic than other areas? Often these questions can only be answered by referring a child like Melanie for an educational psychological assessment, possibly with additional investigations undertaken by a speech and language therapist, along with supporting evidence provided by parents, teachers and medical practitioners (GP, paediatrician and possibly paediatric neurologist). The aim of the investigation or assessment is to ascertain the nature of the problem, i.e. its source, what exacerbates the difficulty and strategies to manage the difficulties and improve the child's access and ability to learn to their fullest potential given the circumstances.

In Melanie's case the psychologist, in conjunction with other colleagues, might wish to consider the following:

- present skills and attainments;
- evidence of 'plateau effect' or loss of skills in recent weeks or months;
- age appropriateness of early development and skill acquisition;
- evidence of new learning since this problem first became of concern;
- if skills are lost, whether the loss is uniform, or whether some are lost while others continue to be gained;
- evidence for day-to-day variations in level of
  a) alertness
  b) performance
  c) memory and retention of skills.

Another example, this time of an adolescent called James, looks at a similar scenario from a slightly different perspective.

James' parents were surprised when they received his end-of-term report from school. They thought he had been doing well. He had maybe been a little tired at home of late, not wanting to go out with his friends on Saturdays as much as he had used to. However, he had given no indication that he had been experiencing any serious problems with his work at school. His report came as a surprise also because up until the last three to four months he had seemed to be coping so well with his epilepsy and the increase in workload at school, caused by his GCSE coursework. Yet here was his report saying that work was incomplete or late being handed in. His teachers were now predicting he would achieve Cs and Ds even in subjects which he had previously always done well. What was going wrong?

In James' case there could be many answers to this question, and the answers might not all (if any) be related to his epilepsy. Many teenagers develop depressive illness or reaction to their epilepsy in adolescence which, after all, is a difficult time of transition without the added complications of coping with seizures. Home problems, issues relating to self-perception and self-esteem, effect on social life, concern and embarrassment over seizures could all contribute to a 'falling off' in academic performance. Changes in seizure pattern, frequency and severity can also occur during adolescence and be exacerbated by the increase in stress engendered by more homework and deadlines to be met. Changes too in medication can upset a person's equilibrium, ability to concentrate, short-term memory, ability to think clearly and rationally about complex problems, process, analyse and retrieve information – especially if it is more abstract in nature. Speed of processing can also be affected. If the student is aware of these problems, they may feel frightened, frustrated and angry as well as powerless to explain them to anyone, let alone deal with them. It is not until academic performance drops, homework is unaccountably late in being submitted – or not submitted at all – or a change in social behaviour makes those around start asking whether something serious is amiss. At such times it is important to take account of the views of the young person's family, subject teachers, form teacher and other significant people in that person's life.

An assessment of cognitive ability is useful as a monitoring exercise and, as in the case of Melanie, to ascertain any disparities in her *profile* of abilities. In particular, one needs to look for hemisphere specific differentiation, i.e. a significant discrepancy between visual (performance) and verbal abilities. This can be done by using standardised intelligence tests such as the *Wechsler Intelligence Scales for Children* (revised UK edition), its pre-school version, *Wechsler Preschool and Primary Scale of Intelligence* (*WPPSI*) or the *British Ability Scales*, all of which are excellent tools for localising brain function and dysfunction in particular areas, or providing evidence for disparities in hemisphere function between the left or right side of the brain. Such evidence, combined with epilepsy-related data such as the focus for the epileptiform discharges which trigger seizures, can provide valuable information on both the cause of the epilepsy (where this is undetermined or unconfirmed), or the impact the epilepsy *itself* is having on the child's ability to learn.

When undertaking such assessments as a psychologist, teacher or therapist, account needs to be taken of:

- seizure type, frequency and severity;
- any changes in anti-epileptic drugs or doses;
- the number of drugs the individual is taking and whether the combination of these has changed;
- the results of investigations concerning the presence or absence of structural brain damage or infection;
- syndrome-specific factors, especially if these are age related;
- problems relating to erratic or prolonged absence from school;
- history of academic achievement;
- whether other areas of functioning are noticeably affected including
    - psychometric skills
    - memory (short term, visual versus verbal, long term, for certain types of information)
    - social behaviour
    - attention
    - motivation
    - perceptual skills
    - information processing (verbal and written).

The psychologist may ask the student to undergo other kinds of test procedures in order to check abilities in these areas. For more psychosocial-oriented issues a clinical psychologist, psychiatrist or cognitive therapist may be asked to contribute to the assessment. A more detailed type of functional assessment of cognitive strengths and weaknesses may be required if the child or young person is being considered for neurosurgery (see Cull and Goldstein 1997 for a more detailed description on pre-surgical assessment and evaluation techniques). Neuro-psychological assessment can also provide supporting evidence of the location of an epileptic focus in the absence of conclusive EEG or neuro-imaging information. Certain types of epilepsy or epilepsy foci have known correlates with specific cognitive impairments. One example of this is the known association between temporal lobe epilepsy (TLE) and memory impairment. Others mentioned in the literature include:

- word-finding difficulties (left TLE more than right);
- face recognition (right TLE);
- face naming (left TLE);
- immediate recall of visual reproduction of drawings (right TLE);
- delayed recall of verbal and visual information;
- impaired phonemic cued recall;
- reading problems (left TLE more than right);
- confrontational naming tasks (left more than right TLE).

Discovering the site of onset of seizures is notoriously difficult using tests of temporal lobe function. Williamson *et al.* (1993) found only a 73 per cent correlation between prediction of laterality of focus in cases with a clear unilateral site of origin. However, it is worth noting that a number of research studies have highlighted the association between complex-partial seizures of temporal lobe origin and memory impairment.

Individuals with frontal lobe epilepsy were also more likely to have memory problems. Other problems noted in *some* people included:

- motor programming difficulties resulting in some forms of dyspraxia;
- initiation and procedural memory difficulties;
- inhibitory mechanisms failure ('think before you speak' routines);
- pragmatic difficulties (lack of understanding of the communicative intentions of others);
- rigidity of thought;
- difficulty in coping with transitions.

Assessment of cognitive decline or uneven loss of skills may require more detailed testing of memory, language conceptual understanding and perceptual development. There are several different types of memory so it is not enough to make a blanket statement such as 'I think Joe is becoming more forgetful.' More forgetful of what? The time? His way around the school? How to get dressed in the mornings? What happened last summer? The major types of memory are summarised in Figure 2.1.

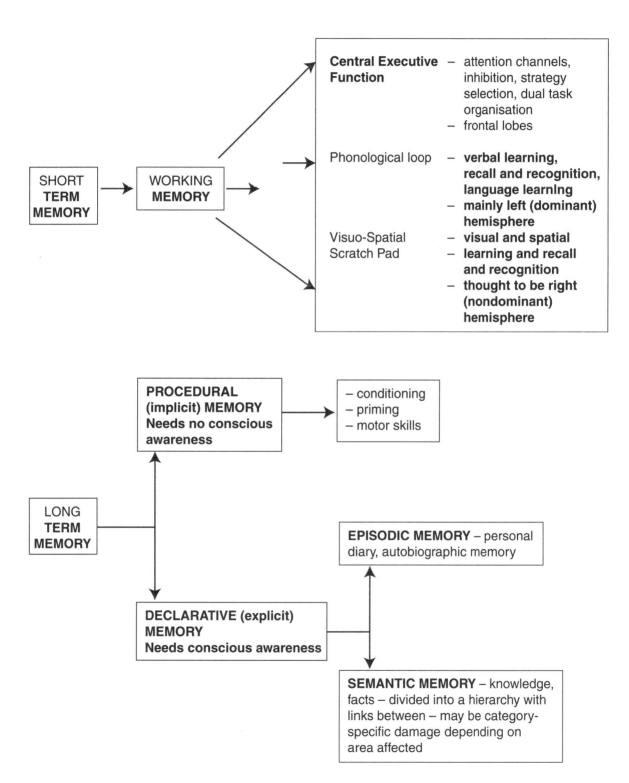

Figure 2.1 Major sub-divisions of memory (adapted from Cromer 1991)

Interpretation of assessment results

Test interpretation should always take into account the following:

- time of day the test was administered;
- whether the child was in a pre-ictal (pre-seizure) or post-ictal (following a seizure) phase;
- if underlying electrical activity in the brain was affecting performance, seen by increased distractibility, general restlessness, poor attention control and possible problems in focusing on visual material and verbal instructions. The person may also look slightly blank or cut off without actually losing touch with their surroundings;
- medication effects;
- previous profile of results, e.g. test re-test deterioration, change in pattern of sub-test scores or emergence of abnormal error patterns in sub-test results.

A fall in overall test score results should not automatically be presumed to indicate genuine skill loss, but might indicate an influence of one of the above-mentioned variables or evidence of slowed learning or plateau effect compared to chronological development. A decision has to be taken as to whether the pattern of scores is delayed or disordered (deviant) and whether this is transient, permanent or 'state dependent' (Fowler 1997). Because no child with epilepsy is ever quite the same, the choice of measurements should be flexible. If necessary the rules of administration may need to be regarded more leniently than in more general use of formal test procedures; for instance in permitting second repetition of a question to be scored that would not be counted under normal circumstances. Error profiles on language tests such as the *Renfrew Word Finding Vocabulary Scales* can tell you more about the nature of a child's word-finding difficulties and whether it is category-specific, instead of simply giving an age equivalent score in the test result.

While results from intelligence quotient (IQ) tests can be useful as a test re-test measurement, they should be regarded as a fairly blunt instrument when deciding on prognosis or intervention strategies. Examination of sub-test results could lead the psychologist or therapist to select more refined or specific tests of functioning in areas giving cause for concern. However, it must be remembered that these are much less stable than the overall IQ. More specific testing is useful both from the teacher's and family's perspective as it can lead to an increased understanding of the difficulties the child is experiencing. It also provides a guide to rehabilitation, intervention and specific learning strategies that need to be put in place to support the child's life both in the community and future learning.

The educational psychologist (EP) is pivotal to supporting and enabling specialised provision, e.g. of Specialist Support Assistant (SSA) support in school, acting as both guide, intermediary and advocate in terms of access to the curriculum. At LEA level, the Educational Psychology Service can advise, inform and indeed influence special needs policy. Old systems and prejudices can often be more effectively challenged if the child and their family have the willing support and commitment from an EP who is well informed about epilepsy-related issues.

At school level, the EP can dispel the negative attitudes and misconceptions that surround epilepsy and, with help from the special educational needs coordinator (SENCO), act as joint facilitator in the inter-agency cooperation so essential with this group of children with mixed needs. In the absence of medical models and protocols to guide staff in the setting up of seizure recording systems, the EP can be useful in helping to devise frequency charts. If required, such records can be linked into behaviour record sheets such as ABC (antecedent, behaviour and consequence recording) charts – important if you wish to examine the relationship between potential behaviour and epilepsy triggers.

Children with more complex health, educational, learning and behavioural needs may need help from a learning support assistant (LSA) for all or part of their school day. While the drive ultimately is for a philosophy of inclusion to be maintained wherever possible, there may need to be compromises made when organising certain parts of curriculum access or management of aspects of the school day, e.g. attendance at assemblies, swimming lessons or school trips. The LSA can prove an invaluable link to a 'real' world to which the child might otherwise be denied full access. The role of an LSA may be a somewhat unusual and demanding one.

We will show later instances of where it has gone wrong. The EP should provide advice and training (in conjunction with the epilepsy liaison nurse) for LSAs on a range of low key but nevertheless important techniques to help them be effective and confident in their roles. In a study carried out by Mencap on the support and training needs perceived by LSAs as important for this purpose, the following were listed as useful to include in in-service education and training (INSET) days or other training sessions:

The role of the educational psychologist

- having the opportunity to train in the relevant subject area(s);
- observation of others 'doing the job';
- going through 'guided' experiences to help them gain in confidence when difficult situations arise, e.g. behaviour difficulties or seizure management in public places;
- knowing where to go for additional information and resources (human, information and material); and
- record-keeping specific to the needs of the child.

At an individual level, the EP might be brought in to advise on setting up monitoring procedures for checking the academic and social progress of children who, because of the nature of their epilepsy and/or the accompanying underlying condition, are regarded as physically, emotionally or psychologically vulnerable. The EP is likely to be called upon to provide evidence of progress in learning and academic attainments, or conversely, loss of newly acquired skills. Above all, however, the EP acts as the pivot, the central point for information exchange, ensuring it is consistently and appropriately shared across a trans-disciplinary framework, which involves statutory agencies, school, relevant professionals and the child's family. As we emphasise in the next section, wherever and whenever possible all this should be done with the parents' help and presence. It is their child. They are living with the 24-hour curriculum and nothing gives greater confidence than involvement.

Impact on the family

In 1999, an investigation for the British Epilepsy Association (BEA) into the effects of both school and home settings on a child with epilepsy was carried out (Johnson and Thomas 1999). Over 50 families who had such a child, their GPs, consultants, school head teachers, SENCOs and teachers were interviewed. The rest of this chapter (and Chapter 3) is based directly on the results of that investigation. The opinions stated are those of the investigators and do not necessarily represent those of the BEA.

As described earlier, epilepsy is a medical condition established by tests conducted at a hospital under the supervision of a consultant, preferably a paediatric neurologist. It is *diagnosed* in the true sense of the word. Generally this process starts when an adult (parent/carer or teacher) notices that there is something wrong. They consult their GP who refers the child to a hospital consultant. The consultant arranges for tests and if the results confirm the GP's suspicions, she/he will prescribe an appropriate course of drugs and pass the case back to the GP for monitoring. The local school health service should be notified and the child's school given advice about day-to-day handling and any likely effects on school activities. Two circulars, one relating to medical conditions and the other to special educational needs govern the in-school support. If the family lives in the right place they may be given the support of a specialist nurse (a Sapphire nurse), initially financed by the BEA.

Epilepsy is a *chronic* condition the symptoms of which, in the majority of children, can be controlled although the condition is not cured. The need for drugs may diminish or disappear in late adolescence. However, in the opinions of the parents in our sample, this occurs less frequently than some consultants would like to believe. It is also a rare condition, therefore few teachers have had personal experience of it. However, because sometimes it can manifest itself in dramatic or unexpected ways, e.g. tonic-clonic seizure or atonic seizure (drop attack), this can lead to fear and stigma being associated with it, essentially due to ignorance of what is happening to the child and how best to cope with it.

Unlike a short-term crisis, such as contracting measles or a broken arm where the expected pattern of 'problem, professional advice, treatment, cure' results, families have to work their way through a learning process that will ultimately enable them to restructure their lives and expectations around the fact of the epilepsy. The experiences during assessment and diagnosis can have a profound effect on how that process turns out.

First contact: the General Practitioner

The local GP is usually the first medical professional with whom parents come into contact when concerned about their child's health. The way in which the GP deals with the consultation and its effects on the parents are influenced by several factors.

First, the GP is faced with an immediate dilemma since each patient is only scheduled to take up four to six minutes of their time. However, for epilepsy 30 minutes has been suggested as more realistic for such a consultation to be carried out effectively. The way the GP deals with this time dilemma is important. Secondly, GPs *always* refer the child to a consultant if they suspect epilepsy. If parents don't realise this, they may believe the GP does not have the expertise needed and is, therefore, not the most appropriate person to deal with their child from then on. Thirdly, it is important to reduce the level of stress that parents feel during the wait for the hospital appointment by discussing with them the process of diagnosis and the possible implications for the future.

Some GPs handled this difficult situation well:

> He just examined her and sort of said, he was pretty sure that it was a fit but he wasn't going to commit himself until she has tests and things done. But he was lovely.

> He said that he thought that it was some form of epilepsy, that Ben was showing the signs that he might have epilepsy, but that to be sure he would have to send us to see Mr Brown so that he could make sure that that was what it was.

This demonstrates a basic level of competence and understanding about epilepsy, and offers an initial diagnosis. The GPs made clear the need to refer to the hospital to confirm this.

Others did not do this:

> Our GP is a really good doctor, you know if you have a normal complaint, but he did not seem to know a great deal about, you know, epilepsy and he even said that he, you know, admitted that this was not his speciality and this was why he was going to send us to see a specialist.

When we asked GPs why they referred children to a more specialised service, some replied:

> Yes, I mean, we just don't see enough cases to be able to justify looking after them properly ourselves. It just isn't on. The investigations and everything need to be run at secondary if not tertiary level, I think. Secondary, certainly.

> I think that's a point more for a neurologist to explore or, you know, a paediatrician. I would expect them to pick up on that kind of thing and really to determine exactly, you know, if it was epilepsy and the investigations required, and the treatment, then to look at that side of things.

Unfortunately, comments made by parents suggest that in most cases the GP does not inform them as to why they are referring their child to another professional. Neither, it seems, do they wish to discuss with parents the numerous possibilities that the symptoms displayed could be attributed to.

> He didn't say why he was sending him for tests and, um and I got really worried and thinking all sorts, sorts of um, could he be looking for a tumour or something like that.

> I went to the doctor because of what the school had told me and I was starting to, you know, get really worried about what could be wrong with her, you know, you know, it could of been something really bad, you know, umm and he just told me that she needed to see a specialist and have tests, you know … no explanation, but (pause) then again I don't suppose I asked.

The next step is the hospital visit. This experience can range from the positive to the traumatic. Specialist children's hospitals handled the situation best but some parents were referred to psychiatric units, or had other investigations such as an EEG in a psychiatric department.

> When we went to this EEG place at [X], we walked in and it was sort of like, like a mental sort of place, and there was like rooms, and there were people wandering around. Um, and sort of the patients were all walking around ... and it was not a nice place to be in at all ... It was very frightening actually. Even though we were walking through it with staff ... and when you've first found out about it [that your child might have epilepsy] it's all a bit, you start to think what effect it will have on his mind, will he end up somewhere like this.[1]

These two sets of parents were referred to an adult hospital and they talked very negatively about their experiences in that environment. However, experiences were far more positive after being referred to a children's hospital:

> The total difference in the staff was amazing, they were so geared up to children and to calm down really frightened parents. It was very good and the consultant was a very good doctor as well.

> And it was a really, the contrast was, when we went to the children's hospital. You couldn't have had a bigger difference; the atmosphere was so, so much better. I mean they were really geared up to talking to John and they had the odd little toys in the room and it was a completely different atmosphere altogether. And I was a lot happier then and John was fine.

Again we found the full spectrum of experiences:

Experience of having tests

> ... the woman who did the EEG, she was just, she was just like Hitler. She was awful, she had no compassion ... she didn't have a redeeming feature about her, she was terrible.

> I wasn't very impressed with her, because she was only young and it is quite frightening. I know it doesn't hurt, but I felt her remarks, such as 'Let's see if there are any brains in your head' were insensitive – Mary took everything literally and was quite concerned about that. I didn't expect that from a professional who was actually doing the EEG. So I think we've had quite a lot of bad.

> Nothing was explained, I mean, no, at the very beginning nothing was explained, was it, because we'd actually seen a programme, hadn't we, on television, about the spike.

[1] In many hospitals the EEG Department is located in the psychiatric unit or department. The GP may not always be able to explain this to the parent or child beforehand as they may be unaware of where the EEG Room is located. Neither will the GP have necessarily seen an MRI or CT investigation taking place. Efforts are being made to make all children's hospital services user friendly and age appropriate. Nevertheless, there is still much room for improvement.

Some parents felt that they had received a reasonable explanation:

> Well the technician sort of explained, I'm going to sit you there and I'm going to push this button, but he wasn't prepared to, um analyse the results. He didn't have the authority; he was just doing the tests. He wasn't obstreperous about it, it wasn't his job.

> The most helpful person we actually came across was the lady who took the EEG at Alder Hey, because she processes so many people and, you know, she was really good. You know, she told us what she was doing, you know.

> Um, and he explained that she showed signs of, because they explained to me that this EEG, would, well that it doesn't always confirm that a child has epilepsy, it can show that they are prone to that like.

> Yes, he explained, like, what goes on in their head, like, when they're either coming up to have a seizure or, and he explained, like, all the different seizures, what they can have, and how it, like, affects them after, and stuff like that. I mean, he was really good, he was really, that part, he was brilliant, like, explaining.

This parent is starting to understand that the diagnosis is a matter of weighing up probabilities. This helps to reduce anxiety. Communicating with parents in their own terms encourages partnership and increased levels of mutual understanding.

Seeing the consultant

The next step is to see the consultant. This is what parents have been waiting for – to find out the best or the worst.

Some parents commented on the language that the consultant used.

> I mean, he could explain these big words quite easily, like, but just someone like a common housewife, like, you know, it's over the top. I think, sometimes I think they ought to talk to you instead of at you.

Some commented on the consultant's attitude:

> Um, yes, Mr, who was the Consultant, I can't think of his name now. Mr ... I can't remember his name. And he sort of looked down on you, you know, sort of, oh you know, parent, paranoid parent sort of thing, you know. Wouldn't explain anything.

> At his attitude, his body language, everything just said it. You know, um, and sometimes I felt so intimidated by that, I didn't ask. We used to come away and I had a thousand things I needed to ask him. Queries I wanted, you know, and things I wanted to say, but I just felt so intimidated. In actual fact, for a long time after we had that sort of fall-out, um, my confidence in myself, as Fiona's mother, was shaken, because I started to think, well maybe I don't know what I'm talking about and maybe there isn't anything wrong with her.

These consultants are defining their role as 'the expert'. They don't see the parents as having a participatory role at this initial, or perhaps any other, stage.

> ... because of the way that he was, he didn't really make me feel like I could ask a great deal of questions, to talk about things, he had spoken and that was it really.

Others were different:

> ... he explained it very clearly to us and whatever questions we asked he answered and continually said to us, you know, whatever you don't take in now, come back to me ... and we felt very comfortable.

> We thought that he was very good because we always felt that we could ask him things, you know little things, that were not really that important, but that we wanted to know for our own peace of mind.

Here the consultant creates an environment in which the parents feel that they have a role to play and that role is participatory in nature. He suggests that they should think about what has been said and see if it makes sense in their family's world. If it does not, or if there are gaps in their understanding, then they are trusted to return and ask questions that will be accepted as meaningful.

Parents' questions to either teachers or doctors should not be seen as being just for the purpose of requesting knowledge and information – they should also be seen as a way of helping the professional understand the ways in which parents are making sense of the situation in which they have found themselves. They should also be encouraged to believe that the rationale and thinking behind their questioning is valid. Sooner or later parents will inevitably develop their own roles; if they feel confident in their experiences and their understanding of them it is less likely that these roles will be confrontational.

Taking an active interest in the questions that they raise will not necessarily result in 'clingy' parents. Most parents realise that consultants have a very heavy caseload:

> And always with the hospital. Sort of you're aware that that's my appointment and I've got an allotted time and they all seem to be under so much pressure.

> I know we have a phone line, but you always think I don't want to call because I know that he's busy and he's not, John's not his only patient.

The most successful mutual exchange of information is achieved through informal liaison with parents. This is a general conclusion that is repeated in the schools' data.

Fortunately some consultants are assisted by Sapphire

nurses, whose job is to liaise between consultant and parents, and other agencies.

Taylor (1994) concluded that specialist epilepsy nurses were viewed, not only by patients, but also relatives, in a positive light. They like the security of having 'someone there' to help them understand and cope with the condition, to discuss and explore medical issues, and wider issues and implications in more depth:

> I think she's just basically, if for some reason the consultant or the doctor doesn't put something so clear, she can come and see the family in their own surroundings, sit down, I mean she's been here for lunch and we go through everything that I've ever been concerned about. Or about us as a family or at school.

> It's just so nice to be able to talk to about all the little things that you are worried about ... She's always there at the end of the phone if I need her, even if it's for something really silly, she always encourages me to call.

Again, the above comments emphasise the importance that parents place on having a real world understanding of the condition and its consequences. They want to chat, talk about the little things even if it's something silly, preferably in their own home.

One of the most worrying things to emerge was the lack of information about drugs. On the one hand taking the tablets should become as routine as cleaning teeth. On the other, the chemicals they contain affect the brain and can have quite severe side effects in some children. Many parents were left in ignorance. They couldn't know whether behaviour was a characteristic of the child, a side effect of the medication, or the manner in which the epilepsy manifested itself. They can also become very confused:

> I mean like, they said there's side effects, and you do think and watch out for the hair loss and things like that.

> The effects of the drugs were, um, talked about so we knew, you know, if we had changes in the drugs that he might be sleepy, and things like that.

It is mainly parents who pass on information to the school. By listening to them a school's level of confidence regarding both drugs and their side effects is increased. The school needs to know what signs and symptoms it should be paying attention to, and reporting to the parents about. The staff can also then identify difficulties with education and learning which may not otherwise be detected.

Well, we started to get really worried about her behaviour, I mean she changed completely, she became really aggressive, no one said this could happen if she took those drugs.

And when it was explained to me that this could cause quite a nasty liver disorder, I took him off it, and made an appointment to see the consultant as soon as possible.

And at no point, at any point were we told about the side effects of medication, they weren't discussed with me. I thought that our consultant, Mr G, would have told me about that if it was a worry. But he tends to be the type of person who always says, 'We'll cross that bridge when we come to it.'

Good communication with medical staff is vital, as other sources of information are not readily available either verbally or in writing:

Didn't get any at all. Only gathered from, literally as I went along. Didn't have any leaflets, no support groups, nothing.

No, nothing really. You see, the thing is, people can tell you things, but it's hit or miss whether you actually take it in, isn't it? That's why literature is so good, because you can come away, and when you've got over the shock of the conversation, you can sit down and read about it.

We found the information not very well forthcoming, you know. Any information we've had, we've really had to fight for. Um, I'm really not sure where the line divides between a petit mal and a grand mal, so it's really difficult to explain to anybody else about it.

This can have a knock-on effect when informing others who have contact with the child. One parent wanted to go to the school to talk to the staff, but lacked the knowledge:

Um, when we found out that he was epileptic, and he was diagnosed, um we went up and explained as best we could, as best we knew, anyway, to the teacher and the headmaster. Um, it was absolutely hopeless, because I couldn't explain to them.

Doctors should talk about the child in ordinary terms and not 'over-expertise' the epilepsy. Parents will be more appreciative if GPs and consultants adopt the same informal approach as the specialist epilepsy nurse. This means talking at a level that parents feel comfortable with, enabling them to convey, in their own terms, issues that they feel they want to discuss. In this way the family can learn to come to terms with the child's condition and be confident about talking to others about it.

What parents would have liked

When talking to parents about their whole experience, in retrospect there were two main points of concern. First, for epilepsy to be fully explained, with practical information about the condition and ways of dealing with it, as the following comments indicate:

> Just what it is and how you go about dealing with it, you know.

> Somebody who could give us, tell us what epilepsy was. You know, just to sort of say, well this is epilepsy, this is how you cope with it.

> But even to have explained what epilepsy was, you know, what might cause it, you know, what we would – I mean, to look for, or anything. We just didn't know anything about it.

> It probably would for me, because I, I've always, I always find it easy if I know exactly what's going on and what everything is, you know. And if, you know, if somebody could sort of talk to you about epilepsy, and tell you all about it and exactly what it is, and everything, you know, it definitely would help I think.

> You know, that's what you needed, really, just someone to say, you know, this is, like, epilepsy is this, this is what happens, this is, like, the result, you know, you can live a normal life. You – you'd have been you know, you'd have got – you'd have got on with life better, really, you know.

> We would have liked to have known exactly, at that moment in time, because I think it would have stood us in good stead to be able to manage Eric's way of life. Because I mean you can't put him on a push-bike, this sort of thing. And it would have been nice to say well, will he be safe to go on a push-bike? What type of fit will he have? Is he safe in front of lights? We've never been told any of this.[1]

> Um so, everyday things, you know, everyday worries. It would have been nice to be able to talk them over with somebody really.

Secondly, people appreciate the security of having 'someone there' to talk to alongside being helped to understand and cope with the condition. As Hopkins and Appleton (1996) indicate, there is an increasing number of appointments for specialist epilepsy nurses. The comments above suggest that parents would have appreciated the services that specialist nurses can provide.

---

[1] Parents clearly need to know from the outset that the effect epilepsy has on the individual concerned, and their family, can be very variable. In the early stages of testing and deciding on a diagnosis and choice of treatment, it can also be difficult for the doctor to appreciate both the immediate and long-term effect on the child and his or her family. Obviously, safety and evaluation of risk need to be discussed, but in the early stages predictions are hard to make. Paediatricians feel it is wrong to place 'blanket' restrictions on children. They would rather work out with the family how risks can be managed and the child enabled to lead as full a life as possible (see later discussion on risk assessment).

Chapter 3

Implications for School, Classroom and Learning

In the past 20 years several documents have been published which affect the way children with special educational needs in England are identified (in more than one sense of the word) and provision made for their needs. A focus of these documents has been the involvement of parents in their child's education. The Warnock Report (DES 1978) and the 1981 Education Act (DES 1981) made parental involvement a central theme, and since that time there has been much discussion of the notion of parental involvement and parents as partners. The *Code of Practice on the Identification and Assessment of Pupils with Special Educational Needs* (DfEE 1994a) also emphasises the importance of collaboration and communication between parents and the professionals involved with the child. Squires *et al.* (1990) point out that parents have a wealth of information about the child that is often not accessed by professionals. If families and professionals are to serve as partners in the assessment process, a mutual awareness of respective skills and attitudes is vital to a successful collaborative relationship (Simeonsson *et al.* 1995).

The Code of Practice is a guide for schools and LEAs on the identification and assessment of pupils with special educational needs. A revised Code of Practice has just been published (DfES 2001). However, while the changes that have been made are important, they are not radical in relation to basic principles. There is still staged progression, although this is now referred to as Support (provided from the school's own resources) and Support Plus (additional resources provided by the LEA). If a child needs help at this latter stage they would normally have a statement of their needs. Under the present Code this must detail each of their needs and state clearly how those needs are to be met. This will usually involve multi-professional assessment by a range of people including a doctor and psychologist, and reports from teachers and support workers. We will, therefore, report in relation to the original Code (DfEE 1994a) as in any case this is the one referred to by our respondents. That Code provides staged assessment, with each stage building on the results of intervention strategies used at the earlier stage(s), progressively drawing upon greater levels of support from outside the classroom. This and the circular *Supporting Pupils with Medical Needs: A good practice guide* (DoH 1996) are the main documents governing the school involvement with pupils with epilepsy.

Most head teachers placed pupils who experienced medical conditions such as epilepsy on Stage One of the Code of Practice as a signal to teachers that they needed watching.

> I would put them on Stage One ... I feel in compiling this list of basic information and sending that round, that had to be creating a small level of awareness, but also concern. And I feel it's safest to put them on a Stage One.

> If for education reasons, that is a factor in a multiple of complex decisions we have to take around learning, behaviour and relationships, that compounds it and it can trigger further things. But the root cause is not because they are per se epileptic.

Translating this from 'senior management speak', his SENCO said:

> Not because they were epileptic, no. Only if we felt it was interfering with their learning progress.

Some would wait for difficulties to arise:

> Not automatically, no. If we felt that behaviour was no problem, the learning was no problem, no problem mixing with the other children, they displayed no emotional problems, then no, I don't think we would.

If a pupil is thought to be having difficulties the parents are supposed to be informed and given information about their rights under the Code of Practice. However, this was not always the case.

> I don't generally inform every parent that the pupil's at Stage One. I would at Stage Two when we're actually intervening and providing something a little bit different, to seek class support, or whatever.

> *When they ask* [our emphasis] they are informed that it really is a marker to say, 'how do you think you are coping?' 'Will it affect your son or daughter's learning?', basically. 'Have you any information you can offer as well?'

Yet the Code states clearly, 'Stage One – at this stage the child's class teacher or year/form tutor consults the child's parents and the child' (DfEE 1994a: para. 2.65). Apart from not fulfilling this statutory obligation, the school is denying itself access to very important information that the family can provide. Parents at another school would be told:

> Right, yes. Well we'd be explaining to them that, you know, as tactfully as we can, because we're at a sensitive area obviously, with parents. But we would be explaining to them that, you know, we're a bit concerned about little Johnny's progress in school and, you know, we're going to monitor it, the teacher is going to monitor it for a term or so and, you know, perhaps we might encourage them to, you know, provide a bit more support at home and perhaps if it's reading or, you know, we'd be sending some, you know, some little bits of homework, depending on what age group they are.

What parents say they were told about the Code of Practice

All this seems rather defensive and even patronising toward parents whose whole, even extended, family life is going to have to take account of their child's epilepsy. They may well have already had to cope with difficulties with doctors. Now they are faced with similar battles at school. The code emphasises the importance of parental participation in collectively deciding the most appropriate way, and the most appropriate level of help that each child needs. Many parents in our survey received little encouragement.

> This new teacher called me in and said that she would like to put John on the Special Needs Register. I said I was not sure whether he was on it, and she said she would find out. She found that he is not bad enough to be Statemented, and he's not bad enough to be on the Special Needs, but he's referred and checked every year, especially now when the epilepsy came up, they just want to keep looking at him and review it.

This parent spoke very negatively about the way that she was told about her daughter needing extra help:

> At one point in the school playground she did actually throw at me that 'I can't Statement Joan because she has just recently had a lot of time off.' Which she had, but then again, um, she had been very poorly and I wasn't sending her to school to be ridiculed. She really wasn't fit enough to go. Um, so I kept her off. And this was the first time that I had any knowledge of her being statemented.

Not much discussion here! How about written information?

> They would have a school prospectus and all the school forms, they would have all that kind of information, I think. Just the general information that the school sends.

There's a summary sheet that goes home with the letter, that explains what each Stage means.

No, it's usually just verbal for Stage One and Two. You see, to give it to parents too early in a procedure, is a bit like flagging out, well you're child's going down this path, bumph. And I would be very worried about doing that, because for most of the children, of course, they don't go down that path.

Some schools said that they would not give parents any written information about the Code of Practice, while others were not aware that there was any such information available. Many said that they felt that written information would formalise the special needs structure too early in the procedure, and this would frighten parents unnecessarily:

I mean we've never given any parents that. I mean, I'm not being funny, but most of our parents would, you know, perhaps I'm being a bit negative here, but I think they'd find that a hell of a lot to wade through, wouldn't they really. So we've not given that out. It would simply confuse them.

Yet the specialist epilepsy nurses commented on the parents' need for information:

My experience with Statementing is that parents are not given enough information, are not given enough guidelines. They're desperate to know what's happening. I think the whole Statementing process leaves a lot to be desired. You're dealing with many different agencies, you're collating and collecting information. I mean the whole process is time consuming. But it's also, I think it's also a very distressing time for families anyway, but they need more information so that they can be helped to understand what is going on.

When talking about the Code of Practice, the specialist epilepsy nurses felt that it was the school's responsibility to inform parents about this structure and support them through it:

Well I think, certainly the school have got to play a role. They don't, but I'm sure they should. They're the people who really should be explaining all this to parents and they aren't. I mean they've Special Needs Co-ordinators in school. It should be part of their role to do that. School nurses could be better informed and also community doctors because part of the process is you have to have a medical, the doctor could make sure that they've got all the relevant information as well. Nobody seems to take it on as part of their role, do they?

Again we find that formal or over-professional approaches are getting in the way of collaboration. We get, 'Stage this and Stage that', 'The process will confuse them', instead of, 'How can we sit down and talk about how you cope at home and what lessons are there for us at school?' Of course parents need to be given information about the Code of Practice. The booklet, *Special Educational Needs – a guide for parents* (DfEE 1994b) explains very clearly the different stages of the Code of Practice and how parents should expect to be involved at these different stages. The vast majority of the schools we talked to did not hold this booklet (some even had to be reminded of its existence) even though it was a free publication, initial supplies of which were delivered to all schools. Parents also need to know to whom they can go for advice. The LEA should give parents the name of such a person: the 'named officer'. Hardly any of the parents we asked seemed to know who or what the named officer's role was.

So if the Code of Practice doesn't help to bring parents and teachers together, do the doctors help? In the UK during the 1950s, it was estimated that up to half of the children with epilepsy were unknown to the school authorities (CHSC 1956). Nearly 40 years later, Brown *et al.* (1993) reported that in at least two-thirds of children with epilepsy the LEA was not aware that they had the condition. The consultants we talked to felt this was no longer the case. Channels are in place to automatically inform the School Health Service so that the educational implications are recognised.

> The information will have gone to the School Health Service, community health to school, school to school, parents to school, so there will be a meeting point, School Health Service tells teacher, then there will be a discussion as to how. The School Health Team will actually give advice to the teacher as to what to do. So there it is – it's coming both ways, hospital in touch, GP in touch, letters from the hospital being available, then the School Health Service also keeps in touch. Nothing is missed out.

Here we can see a touching faith in due process. Notes are completed to be passed on from one area to another, so each set of professionals perceives their role to be complete. As long as the information has been compiled and filed, no further action is needed. There seems to be an underlying assumption that if information is received, people are then better able to deal with, and manage the condition.

However, some consultants admit that even the flow of information is not as effective as it should be, and in some cases the system breaks down and the information never reaches the school.

> When we see a child at clinic, we send a copy to the Community Paediatrician who oversees a number of school doctors, who each oversee one or two schools. It's like sort of feeding it down and now and then it's like Chinese Whispers, and you can imagine, letters often get lost, somewhere in the Community Paediatric path, and never gets down to the school doctor.

What is needed is clear, understandable information relating to the everyday implications of epilepsy for *this*, not some generalised, child. Parents, supported by the Sapphire nurses, seem to be the best people to provide this. As we shall see later, it is only when faced with actual cases does the learning process begin. Before that, the information is inert. Again information necessarily focuses on the condition, not on the life of the child with the condition and the school's response to being a part of that life.

Direct communication between teacher and physician regarding children with epilepsy is extremely rare, yet a hospital-based paediatrician will often follow a child with a chronic condition such as epilepsy from the first few weeks of diagnosis until their late teens. However, there are long intervals between appointments. Sillanpaa suggests that teachers have an important role to play:

> *Teachers are in an excellent situation to identify seizures, particularly non-convulsive varieties, to facilitate diagnosis by describing the overt features and evaluate the efficacy of pharmacotherapy, to report adverse drug effects and to promote the social and emotional development of epileptic children. (Sillanpaa 1983: 664)*

Given that parents/carers are the only people who are consistently present in the child's life, they need to be recognised as the intermediaries. Confidentiality of information regulations such as the Data Protection Act, can inhibit information transfer between different professionals. Sometimes parents need to take the initiative in ensuring that such transfer takes place. There needs to be a continual flow of information between all those involved with the child, which we feel can only be achieved through actually talking to one another. As this is unlikely to be achieved through formal means, every contact, for whatever reason, should also be seen as an opportunity for developing understanding.

Sources of information for schools

In spite of their reluctance to involve parents through the Code of Practice, schools do admit their reliance on them for even basic information.

We are heavily dependent upon the parents for all information, they are the key.

Most schools have their own system for eliciting information about children's health. Usually they ask parents to complete a form when their child starts school:

When a pupil starts at the school, parents are asked to fill in a form and there's a section on that which asks for information about medical conditions. So that's generally where we would get the information. So if a pupil starts in Year 10, there is still that procedure on getting the information.

Unfortunately, this seems, in many cases, to be both the start and the end of the information flow.

> And when he started at the Senior School we had a questionnaire to fill in, if there was any medical problems, so we put on that, 'informed school'. I think that the school should know about anything like that, because of the medication and sports and you know.

As in the health service, there is a tendency for the forms to be filed away and the information not disseminated to those who need to know. Again what parents feel is appropriate to write on a form may be far less than they would convey if they were talking informally to a member of staff face-to-face, or even perhaps within a group. There seems to be a focus on the medication that the child may need to take and the activities in which they can take part – none of which provides information that the class teacher needs to ensure the child's day-to-day access to the curriculum.

Who receives this information?

Once they receive this information, most schools taking part in the research project said that all members of staff, and other employees at school, should and would be made aware of the child's condition.

> Obviously not only teaching staff, because you've got a problem with, as I said to you, the midday assistant has to know what to do, has to know when a child has a fit, what to do if they don't come out of it in a certain time.

The head teacher thought that all staff should be made aware:

> I think we would need to tell everybody, I mean discreetly in the staff meetings because obviously other members of staff will come into contact with that child, for example in the playground on playground duty, or sometimes when the classes share different experiences and so on.

A few schools said that not only would they inform all the staff, they would also tell the pupils at the school.

> And actually, I mean, that has arisen with one last week where the children were made aware of a person's problems and it actually was absolutely vital because she had a seizure on the far side of the playing field where she was, momentarily, out of view of the staff, and the children knew that it was important and they came and got help. And they came, and that was really quite good. So I think it's important that, certainly the immediate class, are aware of the situation.

Unfortunately most comments suggested a 'within-child' condition, and there were very differing views as to whether or not it is something to be kept confidential. Interestingly, schools seemed to make up their own minds about this without consultation with the parents. The focus is on the possibility of the child having a seizure, rather than on the effects it may have on the child and their education. Comments made by parents focus much more on the life-effects rather than the condition itself. This can cause tensions as teachers and parents perceive the condition and the child's experiences at school from a different perspective, resulting in a breakdown in communication leading to mounting frustration. In turn, this can result in misunderstandings. We need a conceptual shift away from 'the problem' to that of a life that accommodates the epilepsy as only one element among others. It could be argued that this is only part of a basic paradigm shift from a focus on an assumed commonality among most pupils to one that focuses on the diversity that exists among them. This, in turn, would also start to break down the clear assumptions of stigma.

Hopkins and Appleton (1996) suggest that teachers should involve children in the class in the care of a child following a seizure. They feel that this teaches children how to help someone who is having a seizure, and provides reassurance that there is no need to be scared or upset when one occurs in their presence.

However, even this limited information sometimes doesn't reach the people who most need it.

One parent said:

> But it's like banging your head on a brick wall. I mean I can't, I wouldn't like to count the number of times I've been to this school, you know, to try and get extra help for her and to explain the problems yet again, to another teacher, who then tells me she will tell everybody else who is involved, and doesn't.

This can result in real disadvantage for a child:

> They said about one of her English tests that her reading age was way below, and they said she didn't seem to be paying attention. And I said, 'You do know that she suffers from epilepsy and she could have been having a petit mal attack.' And they said, 'Oh no, we didn't know.' I said, 'Well, it's down.' They had all this information and, in theory the information is supposed to filter through to every teacher she had, her tutor, etc. etc. I have had grave fears that that ever happened. The theory was there, the practice I don't think was quite so good.

A similar experience was:

> She'd been at this school for three weeks and I said, you know, 'How's she doing with the fits, are you noticing many?', because I was a bit concerned ... And her teacher said, 'What do you mean, fits?' And I said, 'Well, she has epilepsy.' And she said, 'Oh, I didn't know.' So then I had a meeting with her and we went into it in great detail, what happens, and she said, 'Oh, I wondered why she didn't answer me.'

Fortunately it wasn't always like that:

> When he, um, well when he was diagnosed, when he was at Junior School, when he changed to the new school, they said it was absence, this other girl who I spoke to, said the teachers were all aware of it and er, they, you know, they knew they'd to keep an eye on him ... and if they thought that he'd missed anything in a lesson, they would go over it with him.

> Apparently they've got two or three, three or four children who suffer from epilepsy. I don't know whether it's the same sort, epilepsy of some sort. Um, and they're all aware of the outcomes and what they have to do, you know, you – and they're, they're probably over-cautious about Sue having a fit.

Actual experience seems to be the best way of learning, as mentioned earlier. Having had previous pupils with epilepsy at the school, the teachers had gained active knowledge they could then use when a new child came into their care. We are less convinced of the value of information via letters, forms or even conventional INSET without it being complemented by practical, hands-on experience.

Parents' experiences with their child's school were very mixed. Some talked very positively about the school and felt that they had a great deal to thank the staff for because they were proactive in informing and communicating their concerns to them about their child.

> She was falling back in class and it was at the new school that a teacher asked me to stop behind. She thought that Sarah had petit mal. Um, she'd seen it before in another girl in school, a few years earlier. So then we contacted the doctor.

> The teacher put it on her reports that she thought Tamsin was becoming more withdrawn rather than coming out of herself. Because she's very, very shy, anyway. And we were sort of watching it. We just thought it was a character thing rather than anything particular. Then her teacher asked me one day if I'd noticed a change in her behaviour at home, and it was then that we, um, we started to look and we noticed that she was going blank at times.

In the above quotations we can see that in some schools staff engage in informal liaison with parents and, as a result, feel able to disclose their concerns to raise parents' awareness about observations they have made. On the basis of this, parents can then decide whether they need to see a doctor. Schools develop greater partnerships in an informal environment that encourages conversational dialogue between parents, child and staff. Both school and parents gain confidence in each other's ability to share information and to deal with and manage situations in a manner that both parties feel confident and comfortable about.

Where this was happening there was a greater focus on the child's work:

> Well, if they're on medication, what the medication was, if it was something that we needed to be aware of in school because they were taking it in school, or whether it was administered at home. What type of – how it manifests itself, the epilepsy. So to know if they go off into a trance-like – or they just lose attention for a couple of seconds, just something that we can pass on that may affect their work. It may look like a behavioural thing and it's not, so we can actually explain to the staff and the students, really.

And on the individual child:

> I would invite the parents in, to speak to the parents, to find out exactly what the epilepsy consisted of, because it affects each child or each person as an individual. So we would need to know exactly, you know, what is going to happen and when, to the best of their knowledge, first and foremost.

What we are trying to avoid is 'medicalisation'. In the majority of cases it is necessary for a child to take drugs to prevent fits occurring. Taking pills at school was a controversial issue and many schools felt unhappy about it. This is where the health circular referred to earlier is less than helpful: 'There is no legal duty which requires school staff to administer medication; this is a voluntary role' (DoH 1996: para. 11).

While a school is in loco parentis, it should see it as an obligation to do all that is reasonable to ensure that each child in the school has their needs met in as natural a way as possible. Under the current system many parents are required to complete consent forms, making the whole issue very fraught:

> But we have, we do have a form, a consent form that the parents fill in. It's an official form. If a child needs anything for us to administer then they have to fill this form in and supply it with the medicine.

Note the distancing emphasis, 'It's an *official* form.'

> Well the parents have to fill in a form of consent to allow you to give them medicine, then a first aider will administer it.

Again the process is distanced from education by the use of a first aider.

Distancing can be seen once again at this school:

> I would say that one would call for the nursery nurse who is available, and that she would have the necessary medication, and it has to be, had to be approved by the parent, then she would administer it.

The ultimate comment came from the head teacher:

> The policy now is we don't do medicines. If a child is ill, they're off. If they're not ill enough to stay off, they are usually on a medicine that is three times a day, and as we finish at three, they can be 9 o'clock, 3 o'clock and bedtime. Or the parent can come up and administer it. The exception is chronic illness, in which case I administer it. If I am not here, the nursery nurse will. Nobody else touches it. And the other exception, the inhalers are in there.

In the above quotation, the head teacher's comment suggests that if the child needs medication, therefore he must be ill, and if he is ill then he should not be at school. Not only does this approach medicalise the condition, but also results in children with epilepsy being excluded from school thereby restricting the life of one or both of their parents. The whole process is divorced from the real life of the school. The child cannot just take their pills; the medication has to be administered. An essential first step in enhancing the lives of these children is to shift the language of the discourse in schools away from the pseudo-medical and into ordinary speech.

Note: In November 2001 the DFES published a new SEN Code of Practice in which some of the issues referred to above are addressed (see 7.64–7.67 and associated footnote). However, it does not yet appear that the 1996 DFEE/DOH circular has changed and teachers continue to remain in a legally vulnerable state regarding acceptance of responsibility for administration of medication.

The majority of children did not need to take pills/medication at school. However, for those who did, experiences were again mixed:

> So it was an uphill battle from start to finish and the Headmistress wouldn't have her in school over lunchtime, because she didn't, she thought it was a liability. She didn't want to give her medication, and so, you know, we had one problem after another. I use to go backwards and forwards to the school, bringing Jane home at lunchtime to give her her medication and then we had to go back. And consequently because she had a lot off because she was ill, and she'd lost all that time at the beginning. She was short of part of her schooling, was missing out on that as well. And it was tiring her out having to come home at dinnertime. The battles we had.

> No, they won't allow medication in the school, of any kind. She's on anti-asthma medication too, and she's supposed to have that four times a day, but during the school week she only has it three, because they just don't allow any medication in the school.

Parents' comments about giving drugs

Some staff were aware of the possible side effects of medication while others did not seem to be. Understanding ranged from the superficial:

> I can only speak from the one child that I've taught and I was very aware that the medication could make him sleepy and that at times he would not respond as, um, quickly, as he, I would expect, but it didn't really seem to be a big problem.

Knowledge about the side effects of medication

to the quite sophisticated:

> Well I suppose there's two aspects to that. There's the actual medical condition, which may be the epilepsy and the effect that that would have, you know, whether he was having petit mals and was blanking off and wasn't, if you like wasn't receiving, wasn't receiving that day, or that period of time, because I believe it's a short period of time, isn't it, you know. And it could be the effects of the drugs as well. So there are, you know, two sides to that.

It is essential that staff are aware of the possible side effects of medication, in terms of both educational implications and possible changes in the child's behaviour, so that the change in the child is not misinterpreted as being something else, e.g. laziness. Information should be aimed at demystification. We are not talking about hard drugs, just pills that a child has to learn to take to control their condition in the same way that they need to learn to brush their teeth or remember their glasses.

We recognise that when you first meet it, epilepsy can be both frightening and frustrating.

> You know, you feel like, OK you've been told something and certain information, but you think well, should I know more? You know, you feel a little bit in the dark and it's a bit of a worry, you know, if someone's going to have a fit in the classroom, or they're going to have, you know, something's going to happen, or suddenly an asthma attack.

> Well I mean I asked his mum what we should do, and sort of spoke to her a few times, and when he sort of didn't have any, it became a lot easier. But it was still the fear of not knowing what to expect that worried us.

But once you have survived the first experience:

> It's certainly been a learning process for us, I think, which we have gone through and I think that it has raised our level of awareness, in terms of possible future pupils.

> It's like you learn as you go along. I mean until Wayne I hadn't taught anyone with it before. If it happened again I think that I would be more relaxed about being able to cope with it.

Parents really can help:

> We didn't realise at even the outset, we did not realise, you know how much we needed to learn about the condition. I mean we knew the basics but with mum's help we learnt to deal with it, and knew what to expect.

And boys will be boys:

> We learned to distinguish between a real fit and a pseudo fit. Because, as most teenagers, he clicked 'If I don't want to do that, if I have a fit, I'm out of it.' So he was having quite a few.

It is only when schools actually experience having a child with epilepsy that it becomes a way of life for the staff. One way that teachers might get this experience, albeit artificial, could be through epilepsy workshops. However, this must be done 'for real'. They need to have a pupil in mind, preferably with the parents there to make it part of their active knowledge. This would be of far greater value than all the pre-admission questionnaires.

A second factor involves the way in which the school is told about the condition. Comments that parents make suggest that it is not enough for a letter to be sent to the school giving an explanation. Neither is it enough for parents to go to the school and discuss it with the staff. It is only when someone whom the staff perceive to have relevant expertise in this area actually visits the school, to talk to them in person about the condition, its management and possible implications, do the staff begin to feel more confident in their ability to deal with the situation in the school setting. The following comment illustrates this very well:

> They did phone quite often with every slight thing, but again I think when the Sapphire Nurse had a word with them, I think they relaxed more, that I didn't have to be called if he'd fallen over.

In terms of what happens when a child has a seizure, schools feel that they take parents' wishes as being a central concern.

This head teacher said:

What happens after a seizure at school?

> We had a standing arrangement that we would phone them if there were problems. And they came to collect him on a few occasions as well.

Another said:

> It would depend from, I mean generally they're allowed, you see the school nurse would know what to do in most cases. And if it's a case of yes, we know this is happening, or we'd phone the parents and we allow them to sleep it off, and the parents make a decision about whether to come and collect them or not … that's how it's been handled in the past.

Again:

> Thinking about the individual cases in the school, it probably would depend on the parents' wishes. And the student. That has happened on one occasion, I know, when both the child and the parents wanted her to stay in school, and she did. I think, generally, that we would insist that they went home.

> It would be more than likely that parents would be contacted straight away and they would be taken home.

However, some of the comments that parents made suggest that they did not want their child to be sent home after they had suffered a seizure.

> If she was bad, then they'd ring for us to pick her up, which was okay, but sometimes I thought that maybe it would have been better had she slept at school and then she could have gone back into class and carried on.

> They dealt with it, but they wanted me to come and take him home. But, it, it would be nicer if they would allow him to sleep it off in the medical room, but I think, I don't know whether they feel they're vulnerable that way, or what, I'm not sure.

> He usually sleeps in the classroom because they haven't got a medical room. So he sleeps in the quiet corner and then joins the class again after about fifteen, twenty minutes.

This parent talked about the practical difficulties of always being expected to go and pick her child up from school following a seizure:

> They would always ring and ask me to go and pick her up. I can understand why they wanted that because there wasn't really anywhere that she could go and sleep it off, but at the same time it made it really difficult for me because every time I went to the shops I would be thinking, oh what happens if they ring and I'm not there.

One of the specialist epilepsy nurses also commented on the difficulties that parents face when the school expect them to take their child home after a seizure:

> The parents don't even feel that they can go shopping, they have to be by the phone at all times. Um, I have tried to address this with the schools, that perhaps all the child needs is to sleep in a corner of the classroom to recover. But, it's a major problem for some families. I've not found the ideal solution really for this.

From the comments made above, we can see a discrepancy between schools' perception that they are doing what parents want, and what the parents actually do want. The act of sending the child home after a seizure once again suggests that schools perceive the child as being ill, consequently they should not be in school, rather than seeing the child as having a condition and the seizure merely a symptom of that condition.

Lack of understanding about the condition

Experience of dealing with a number of schools indicates that teachers, and sadly, members of the School Health Service, still view epilepsy as a simple construct of major and minor seizures, with very little knowledge about its many differing forms, both clinical and sub-clinical, which may be constraining the growth of learning and behaviour in children (Scrambler 1990). Comments that some parents made support this and indicate that some staff lack a full understanding of the child's condition and how it manifests itself, despite their assertions to the contrary. Parents felt that they had told the school about the condition, but they still did not seem to understand it. This issue was also talked about by one of the specialist epilepsy nurses, as she explained:

> Very often schools see a child who has absence seizures. You know, they think, there's no problem here, because the seizures aren't dead dramatic, there's no problem and yet they're not aware that, you know, the child is totally unconscious at this point, therefore there is a problem that needs to be looked at and monitored. Some schools see it not as a problem at all.

Comments parents made support this:

> Well they, I don't think they realise that there's all forms of epilepsy. They just put it down to ... they just thought she'd be thrashing around on the floor, or something, sort of thing, they don't realise that there are absences and things like that. They're very naive.

Even after explaining to the school about her daughter's absences, this parent felt that the school had no understanding about the condition that she found very frustrating:

> Her teacher said she wouldn't be so bad if she didn't day-dream quite so much, you know, if she paid more attention she'd get more out of it. And I'd say, 'Well do you not think perhaps that this is, you know, the epilepsy?' And she said, 'Oh, I don't think so dear, we would have noticed that.' This is the attitude we used to have. And I'd say, 'But that is how it manifests itself, you know.' Oh, you know, I was so exasperated I just couldn't get through.

When talking about her daughter's education, this parent did not feel that the school had been much help. Neither did they understand her condition:

> We reckon that she probably missed two years of her, not two years of her education, but with, and this switching on and switching off, we didn't actually know how often it was happening. The school weren't much help, I have to say, this school here that we sent her to, even though we have told them this fact they still say that she often doesn't pay attention and that she day-dreams sometimes, so what can you do?

Again, a similar experience was recalled by this parent:

> Well, and because the teachers had got used to him, if he was having a petit mal at the back of the class, so he just sat there like that. They didn't notice because Mark was just sat there. They did not notice, so therefore he'd come home from school and when he was up there a lot of his school books had half a page of work and then nothing for about three pages.

Another told of an incident that clearly shows that the school had no understanding about the condition at all, an incident that must border on child abuse:

> Yes she's had two lots of detention because she had fits at school, one in the playground at school. Her teacher gave her a red card because she was slumped up against a wall, and when the whistle was blown, she didn't respond. And because she didn't respond for two minutes the teacher left her, she got everyone into line, and because she still hadn't responded she gave her a red card. And she started shouting at her and of course she eventually started coming out of the fit, and um, couldn't understand why everyone was shouting at her, and just went hysterical.

These comments suggest that when seizures are not dramatic then the fact that the child has epilepsy temporarily disappears from the teacher's consciousness. Stores (1979) suggests that this may result in the child's change in behaviour being misinterpreted as either not paying attention, day-dreaming, being lazy and numerous other explanations for which the child may be reprimanded. A study of children with epilepsy conducted by Holdsworth and Whitmore (1974) found that their teachers described 42 per cent of pupils with sub-clinical seizure activity as 'markedly inattentive' (see page 60 for an explanation of 'sub-clinical'. Inattentiveness, in turn, was associated with unsatisfactory educational progress and with difficult behaviour. The comments that parents made highlights the difficulties that teachers can encounter when behaviour such as absences do not manifest themselves in a way that can be defined clearly as normal or abnormal. However, this is not to say that in certain circumstances children may display false absence seizures for one reason or another. Teachers must remember not to automatically make this assumption – they need to determine the true nature of the episode. We suggest that teachers would benefit from receiving an 'ordinary' explanation about the condition in order not to over-medicalise it.

Experiences that parents recounted suggests that the questionnaires they completed at the start of school ask general questions about their child's condition. They did not ask specific questions about how the condition manifests itself in that particular child, this information being vitally important for any class teacher. Teachers need to be clear and sensitive about the nature of absence seizures, how they manifest themselves and their implications on learning. This is a subtle matter that requires a good deal of confidence on the parts of both parents and child, and requires staff to talk to and with parents about their experience of the condition and strategies they use to come to terms with it.

Attention control has been shown by some researchers to vary according to seizure type (Hermann 1991; Piccirilli *et al.* 1994). On the whole, sustained attention was found to be most important in children with predominantly generalised seizures. Tasks requiring selective attention, e.g. laboratory work, were more likely to be affected in children experiencing frequent or clusters of focal (partial) seizures.

Comments made by most of the parents suggest that they would like to work collaboratively with staff in order to gain information about medical and educational developments of their child. However, it seems that the school does not always reciprocate this:

> He was having a few [seizures], we asked at the school if they'd keep a record for us because they saw him more through the day, so that we could tell, but they never bothered.

This parent talked about a similar experience. Due to a change in medication, she wanted to know if there were any changes in her child's behaviour at school in order to monitor and record developments:

> And she was falling asleep in the playground or at her desk, or things like that. They would just leave her. They wouldn't tell me they'd been happening or anything, other children would tell me these things had been happening. You know, when we had them back for tea, and things like this. And then I'd go in and ask and the teacher would say, 'No she's been the same as usual really.' Because I needed to know, because at that time they were still trying to adjust the medication. It was obviously affecting her entire life and I needed to know these things.

Another parent said the school had agreed to complete a weekly report so that the school and the parents could monitor the child's progress at regular intervals:

> They were supposed to do this weekly report for us, but we haven't had it, I've had it once and then that's been it nothing since then.

In contrast, some parents felt that schools were very cooperative and more than willing to pass on information:

> The school were very good, you know, when she had time off and things like that. If she had been ill in the night I could go into school and ask the class teacher what they had been doing so that I could help her to catch up with the work, and Mrs D would be more than willing to tell me what they had been up to you know.

Another parent also felt that the school wanted to be involved and was willing to give information:

> They were good like with things like. If he'd been badly behaved at school they would tell me, not in a horrible, um you know way, because I had asked them to tell me if he was naughty at school, like he was naughty at home.

Lack of cooperation

It is apparent that the parents in this sample were keen to pass on information to the school about their child's condition. It is equally important that schools also try to provide parents with the information that they require to understand the condition further. It is only through an informal two-way communication system that both parents and staff can gain a better understanding about the condition and the way it manifests itself in that particular child.

Comments from another parent suggest that although the school was willing to cooperate, it had difficulty doing so because staff lacked sufficient knowledge about the condition itself to understand the reason for the special consideration her child needed:

> Yes, I explained why I needed to know [about recording the seizures] and they said, oh yes, you know, they were very, very pleasant and trying to accommodate, but they hadn't got a clue what I was talking about, why I needed it.

Working collaboratively with parents can lead to greater partnership between parents and school. This is something that all schools should strive for. If parents do not feel that schools are willing to work in collaboration with them, the consequences can be detrimental for the child. Parents are then less likely to communicate valuable information to staff.

Negative perceptions of school

Some parents talked negatively about their child's experience at school. One parent said:

> Um, the school weren't much help, I have to say, this school here that we sent her to.

> They just kept putting her back a class, and putting her back. And they were holding her back really, I could see it, so I wasn't happy with it and I went in and said 'I'm not happy with the standard of education she's receiving here.' Um, because she was going back, obviously, and she was getting bored anyway, being with the same teacher and the same pupils, or at least, younger pupils, younger children.

Positive experiences of school

Some parents felt that the school was very good with their child and talked positively about their experiences:

> Mrs D was absolutely brilliant. She'd meet me after school, in her own time, and she would coax Joan into the classroom, she would ring her up at home and say, 'Come on, I'm waiting for you. Are you coming to see me?' And Joan would go. And she was very tolerant, wasn't she, um and she said, 'Do you think we ought to Statement her?' So, we started the first stages, we filled in some forms, but it never actually went ahead.

The staff from school were lovely about it, weren't they? They rang home about it, and the, some of the children had been quite upset, obviously, to see her having a fit and, um, the year tutor, just sat them all down and said, 'Look this is it. You've got to be nice with Brenda.'

I've got an absolutely brilliant class teacher at the moment, he is brilliant. Um, in this class they're now going to start going swimming, and I was terrified because obviously she's got to have a one to one watcher. And, um, I went in to see him about it, and we – my husband was there, and he said, 'It's all right, it's already organised.' So there's no problem there. So we're just waiting now for them to actually start swimming.

This parent was happy with the school:

They were fine, yes. The first teacher she had there was brilliant, she asked me if I could take a little picture of Alice in so that they could put it on the staff room notice board, so that the other teachers would recognise her, which I think was very nice. That was reassuring. Um, when Alice went into the Juniors, that would be her second teacher, um, they rang me up about the swimming, you know, to check that I had no problem with her going swimming.

Compare this with the schools that seem to want to shroud epilepsy in some sort of secrecy.

I've never really met any negative attitudes. Most of the teachers have been pretty good. Most of them have obviously said, 'What are we to expect?' And luckily, when she went into, like Junior School, even though we'd moved to a different area, one of the supply teachers who'd been at her Infant School was then in the Junior School, and she suffered from fits herself. And Jen found that she could go and talk to her to find out more, you know. Because she's never really known anybody else, apart from that one teacher, who's actually had fits.

Excellent. They forget it – it sounds awful that. But they don't forget because they know it's there, and that's that.

As with the doctors and hospitals, schools need to recognise that when dealing with a pupil who has epilepsy they are dealing with the pupil and not the epilepsy. Their full inclusion in the class and school should not be a problem. The parent usually has all the information they will need about the condition, its effects and how to deal with them. All the strategies our parents reported from schools with which they were satisfied are just simple, thoughtful responses to an individual child's needs. Fear and prejudice are the barriers. Openness, personal and mutual regard are the attitudes that engender successful partnerships.

Chapter 4

Access to the Curriculum – A Whole-School Approach

Inherent in the introduction of the National Curriculum was the philosophy that all children would have access to a range of core subjects, regardless of any disability or difficulty that had previously excluded them from participation. To enable access to take place the curriculum may need to be adjusted to allow for the pupil's *style* of learning and one that meets the *needs* associated with supporting the management of their epilepsy within the school environment. Joining in with physical activities, going on geography field trips, participating in school trips and outings are the obvious areas that we think of when considering curriculum access. This is particularly relevant when staff become increasingly concerned about health and safety related issues. Often, exclusion rather than inclusion seems the easiest, cheapest and safest answer. Nevertheless, with current and forthcoming government legislation in mind, schools should strive to include children with epilepsy in all aspects of the National Curriculum. Indeed, the new National Curriculum document (DfEE 1999) states clearly the three principles of inclusion:

- Setting suitable learning challenges
- Responding to pupils' diverse learning needs and
- Overcoming potential barriers to learning and assessment for individuals and groups of pupils.

The role of the SENCO is pivotal in both collecting and disseminating information about the child or young person's condition. Fear of including a child in a subject area or activity can be allayed by appropriate information about:

- what to expect;
- what to do;
- who to notify;
- how to cope;

along with strategies and guidelines which address:

- subject-specific access – environment;
- subject-specific access – information transfer;
- level of risk;
- realistic expectations of the child's overall potential and day-to-day learning (see Chapter 3).

Many children with epilepsy – with or without additional learning, sensory or physical difficulties – are known to suffer a sense of frustration and/or low self-esteem because of the nature of their epilepsy. Teachers can actively seek to improve the child's view of him/herself both as an individual and in relation to his/her peers, by engendering a positive philosophy of inclusion across all areas of the curriculum. This may be achieved in a variety of ways. Across the school there should be a policy of:

- positive promotion of attitudes towards students with disabilities – particularly those with 'hidden' or 'unseen' disabilities which can sometimes be harder for peers to accept;
- encouragement of an atmosphere that nurtures high expectations, high quality planning and (where needed) professional support on an individual basis;
- encouragement of (and allowance for) reasonable risk-taking within specified subject/activity areas.

Academic subjects

Obviously the level of risk-taking is reduced when the pupil is being educated in a static, predictable environment. However, there are certain methodological implications that teachers and students would benefit from when planning a whole-class or an individual education plan (IEP) approach to subject teaching.

Students with epilepsy benefit from formality of routine and structure when being presented with information. Teachers need to bear in mind that epilepsy is a *symptom* of an underlying problem in the pupil's brain that can affect the following:

- acquisition (taking-in of information), especially if this is presented in chunks;

- retention, processing, categorising and prioritising of the assimilated information;
- formulation and expression (verbal and written) of an appropriate answer.

Providing a structured framework, a routine in which to locate the information, helps to anchor the student in what can appear to be a frustrating and sometimes fragmentary process of information-processing. The following will help to ensure information is assimilated:

- present information in short chunks;
- reinforce verbal information with written notes or bullet-pointed hand-outs;
- offer direct support when the pupil is felt to have difficulty in maintaining a focus of attention – particularly when working in group settings.

There is an increasing demand for homework at both primary and secondary school level. The workload becomes significant when the pupil is required to produce coursework for GCSEs, NVQ units and in a more academically formal way, for A level and AS level work. Pupils should generally only be exempted from examination or coursework under the following circumstances:

- If they have had a major seizure, i.e. a tonic-clonic, atonic, complex partial seizure which has developed into a tonic-clonic seizure, prolonged or atypical cluster of absences or other seizure types that have affected their level of consciousness or after which they needed to sleep.
- If there is a prolonged alteration in level of consciousness, alertness, general well-being, mood stability characteristic of a warning that a seizure is expected (pre-ictal).
- If sub-clinical activity is suspected. This term refers to a state of increased electrical activity in the brain due to the child's epilepsy but which is not of a degree, focus or intensity to manifest as an obvious seizure. Such periods can have a marked effect on one or more of the following:
  a) attention control
  b) short-term memory (usually temporary in this context)
  c) self-composure
  d) mood
  e) behaviour
  f) tolerance of light and ambient noise.
- Significant change in treatment within 24 to 72 hours prior to the homework being set or expected attendance at an

examination. The change may include an increase, decrease or withdrawal of medication. Such changes should be avoided wherever possible if the pupil is due to submit important pieces of coursework, take an examination or undergo a formative assessment of some kind, e.g. a unit evaluation in the presence of an external examiner, or an attainment test.

If a pupil persistently uses epilepsy as an excuse for non-submission of homework or coursework, then the matter should be taken up initially with the student. Parents should be consulted in their role as partners with the school to ensure the student is given the best possible opportunity both to participate and achieve the most from completing the necessary work, examination or test.

Key Stage test and formal examination arrangements

The Joint Council of the Examination Boards provides advice on special arrangements for children with various conditions and disabilities. They give specific guidance for children with hearing and visual impairments, learning disabilities and dyslexia. There are also guidelines for those under SEN provision. Arrangements include:

- extra time (usually on a ratio per hour basis);
- rest breaks;
- stopping times (similar to rest breaks but can be unscheduled);
- early opening of papers arrangements (mainly for when students with visual or hearing impairment need to have papers transcribed into a different format).

There are arrangements in place to allow for flexible working in Key Stages 1, 2 and 3 assessments (details available from the Qualifications and Curriculum Authority (QCA) – see Useful Addresses/Internet Sites). Further work is currently being undertaken to modify and improve the assessment and reporting procedures. Details can be found in 'Assessment and Reporting Arrangements' for each Key Stage, published annually by the QCA in conjunction with the Department for Education and Skills (DfES) and *Excellence in Schools* (DfEE 1997b) (copies available from QCA Publications). However, the emphasis continues to be placed on an open framework which will be teacher/student led, i.e. the teacher applies for exemption or allowance for extenuating circumstances to be applied during a particular assessment. Similar arrangements are in place in Wales and Northern Ireland (see Table 4.1).

Examinations and assessed work

As previously mentioned, many children with epilepsy have attention control problems and find it difficult to focus on test and examination work for more than short periods of time. Others may be at increased risk of having seizures in stressful situations. Some pupils may be prone to having seizures at certain times of day which can be allowed for within the standard school timetable but not when formal examinations are in progress. For such children it is often advisable to arrange

September	School asked for numbers of year 6 children and teachers and optional tests ordered for years 3, 4 and 5.
October	Arrangements booklet sent out to schools.
November	Schools receive tests order forms. This order includes options to order specialised test scripts for HI and VI children.
December	Details to be returned to the Schools Co-ordinations Unit (SCU).
January	Tests ordered for use in years 3, 4,and 5 arrive, together with a current Key Stage 2 standards report.
February	Deadline for schools to make requests for special arrangements to LEAs or QCA.
April	Schools notified of decisions/arrangements for 'special circumstances'. Schools receiving external marking arrangements, Guide and Associated documentation.
May	National Curriculum tests (including modified tests) arrive. Tests take place on timetabled days. Test scripts and mark sheets are sent to the external examiners.
July	Return of test results for each child plus a Level Threshold Tables booklet from QCA. Schools' teacher assessment results submitted for the purpose of national data collection. Mailing reviews completed where relevant.
By end of Summer term	Schools will now have reported results to parents following guidelines laid down in the Assessment & Reporting Arrangements booklet for Key Stage 2.
21st September	All marking reviews by external agencies are now complete.

Table 4.1 Modified example of Key Stage 2 administration and statutory assessment timetable

for the test or examination to be taken in a separate room or away from the school. In such cases it might be helpful for the pupil to sit the examination in their own home, another institution – maybe a smaller unit attached to another school – or in hospital if the child is unwell. Providing the following conditions are met, there is no need to seek permission for making specific accommodation arrangements provided that:

a) the test takes place according to the timetable laid down by the statutory authority;
b) although the examination time may be interrupted for 'rest breaks', the total time allowed remains the same as under normal circumstances;
c) security and confidentiality of material is adhered to; and
d) the invigilator is not a relative of the candidate.

Emergency permission may need to be sought if the pupil has a seizure unexpectedly within the period of the examination or within a period of time, e.g. 12 hours prior to the examination when it is felt that the pupil's performance would be adversely affected to a significant degree. The head teacher is responsible for notifying the LEA or examining board of any emergency arrangements required.

The Joint Council for General Qualifications (see Useful Addresses/Internet Sites) publish a comprehensive booklet produced each September, *Regulations and Guidance Relating to Candidates with Particular Requirements*. Epilepsy is not specifically singled out as an issue per se, nevertheless the awarding bodies in the consortium recognise:

> 2   that there are some candidates who have coped with the learning demands of a course, but for whom the standard arrangements for the assessment of their attainment may present a barrier. This applies both in the case of candidates with known and long-standing learning problems and candidates who are affected at or near the time of assessment. Such barriers may arise as a result of:
>
> 2.1 a permanent or long term disability or learning difficulty
> 2.2 a temporary illness, disability or indisposition
> 2.3 the immediate circumstances of the assessment.
>
> (Joint Council for General Qualifications 2002: 2)

Compensation can be given in the light of *special consideration* of the illness, indisposition or disability of the candidate in relation to 2.2 and 2.3 whereas *special arrangements* (see earlier in relation to guidelines) need to be put in place to take account of 2.1. Special consideration is only given when certain circumstances arise *at* or *near* the time of the examination that were not catered for by the making of prior special arrangements. Supporting evidence for some arrangements may be required from the child's GP, paediatrician or paediatric neurologist. They may be required to confirm the age of onset, length of time and current state of the child's epilepsy. They may also be asked to give details of current treatment and whether there have been any recent changes in its management that might have a bearing on academic performance.

Other evidence may be required in the form of recent assessment or in relation to SEN provision, by an EP and/or other therapists or specialist advisory teachers. Details of who is able to provide such evidence are given in the *Regulations and Guidance Notes* (published by the Joint Council for General Qualifications). (Further information can be found in the physical disabilities and learning difficulties (including neurological dysfunction) sections in the chapter dealing with guidance for particular disabilities.)

Practical subjects and laboratory-based work

Many teachers and school management teams etc. are naturally anxious about placing a student whom they feel to be at risk of self-injury in what might be perceived to be a vulnerable or dangerous situation. The situation is more acute when:

- the student is known to experience seizures without warning;
- the student has atonic or drop attacks which are known to occur suddenly and can cause head, facial or other injury;
- the student is handling dangerous substances, e.g. inflammable or corrosive liquids or equipment that might cause burns.

While those working with students with epilepsy must demonstrate that they have taken reasonable precautions to ensure the student's safety, those involved need to take account of the following when seeking to provide the highest standards of achievement in the students and when working under, at times, somewhat constricting circumstances:

a) The five guiding principles as set out by the QCA (2000),
   i   the inclusion of all learners at relevant levels of activity
   ii opportunities for continuity and progression for all learners
   iii achievement of the highest possible standards for all learners

 iv the recognition of achievement of all learners

 v the provision of easily accessible advice and guidance for all learners;

b) the likelihood of a seizure occurring (many seizures only happen at certain times of thc day, week or month);

c) the type of seizure that is most expected;

d) whether the person is at risk of losing consciousness or experiencing impaired awareness of the surroundings and for how long;

e) the level of supervision required to meet the perceived risk.

(See also the Education Act 1997 Part V, Chapter One, Paragraph 26 (QCA 2000) and the Education Act 1996 Part IV (Special Educational Needs) and the BEA website (see Useful Addresses/Internet Sites) for up-to-date information on relevant education legislation.)

Working through planning and catering for such eventualities within teaching assessments or therapy sessions is known as conducting a risk assessment. Many of the issues considered in relation to practical subjects will also need to be addressed when planning access to participation in physical education (including outdoor pursuits and swimming).

Physical education, outdoor pursuits and swimming

As in other areas of the curriculum, the more knowledge the teacher or other professionals, support assistants etc. can gain about the nature and management of the student's epilepsy, the better for all concerned. The main area of contention (especially with the student) is that of climbing, abseiling and similar activities involving height. It is important in such instances to draw up definitive guidelines with the consent of all concerned. The guidelines should clearly stipulate when certain activities are (and are not) permitted and the appeal procedure should any of the people involved be unhappy regarding a decision to exclude the student from an activity – either temporarily or permanently. Parents may need to sign an individually drawn-up consent form – again to ensure agreement about the nature and degree of risk to which the student is permitted exposure.

It is a commonly held view that children with epilepsy are not advised to go swimming. Providing proper precautions are taken there are no reasons why a child with epilepsy may not go swimming, although scuba diving, jet skiing and similar activities are not advised without first seeking informed medical consent.

One way around maintaining constant supervision while the child with active epilepsy is engaging in an activity such as swimming is by adopting a 'buddy' system – one of the child's friends is encouraged to stay by them during the activity to ensure they are kept under supervision. It is important that the child with epilepsy is not over-protected, or singled out as someone special or different, yet is encouraged for social, emotional and health-related reasons to join in as many activities as possible. For the child with simple partial seizures, or one who only has seizures at night or whose epilepsy is completely controlled, constant supervision is not so high a priority.

Guidelines on recognition of a seizure in water should included warnings to pool staff to be alert to:

- inappropriate or unexpected change of direction of the swimmer;
- the child does not respond to their name when called;
- the child's stroke may become uncoordinated or cease altogether;
- their arms, legs or head may start to jerk or stiffen involuntarily;
- a cry from the child.

When the child starts to have a seizure approach them from behind or to the side, making sure that a flailing arm does not knock you off balance. Hold their head gently but firmly, ensuring it keeps clear of the water while the seizure is in progress. Sometimes, using a float under the head can help keep it out of the water during the seizure. As soon as possible guide the child to the side or shallow water and seek assistance to lift them onto the side of the pool. If the seizure continues or they go into another seizure, turn them on their side and place something soft (a folded towel) under the head to prevent injury.

If the teacher or group leader does not feel happy or confident enough to cope with the potential for this situation to occur – particularly in the primary school – arrangements can sometimes be made for a parent to come to provide psychological and physical support until the routine of the session becomes established.

All lifeguards and poolside attendants should be made aware that the group contains a swimmer with epilepsy. Check they are trained to cope with a person having a seizure while in the water.

Today there are still schools and local authorities that will not permit children and young people with epilepsy to engage in physical leisure and school-based activities on their premises.

Support and information can be provided by other agencies such as the epilepsy liaison nurse, GP, National Society for Epilepsy and local branch of the BEA (see Useful Addresses/ Internet Sites). Such information can allay fears of mismanagement (perceived or otherwise). It also ensures that the correct policies, procedures and guidelines are laid down with named or designated people included, so if a child has a seizure, every eventuality is catered for. They are then able to be included and share in the same activities as their friends and peers (as is their human right), and not excluded because of our own fears and ignorance.

Chapter 5

Epilepsy and Behaviour

In individuals with epilepsy as a symptom of an underlying condition (which may or may not be precisely known), there may also be signs of behavioural disturbance. The changes in behaviour, or presence of difficult or problem behaviours can be either temporary – hours, days or weeks – or more long term. The most common questions asked by parents, carers, teachers and other professionals involved with the young person are 'Is the behaviour caused by the seizures?' and 'If the seizures become controlled will the behaviour go away?'

There are no straightforward answers. Certainly there are times when a change in behaviour is seizure-related. However, there are other instances when a 'learned' behaviour can be the main problem support staff need to deal with, or it may be that the behaviour is part of an underlying condition in the brain which has given rise to both the epilepsy and behaviour difficulties – and sometimes problems in other areas such as learning too.

We need to examine whether such behaviours are associated with the following:

a) particular seizures;
b) time of day, e.g. early morning, when hungry or over-tired;
c) are context-related (social, learning, activity associated);
d) mark the onset of illness or infection;
e) are linked to stress, fatigue or hunger;
f) another condition such as autism;
g) a sign of a new problem such as a depressive illness;
h) a non-epileptic attack disorder;

or associated with environmental factors not covered in c) which are more person-centred, e.g. frustration, boredom, low self-esteem or unhappiness.

It can be difficult to work out exactly what is triggering the behaviour given such a range of options from which to choose. The following example illustrates this point.

Martin was a friendly and outgoing boy aged eight years. His work in school had been unremarkable until recently when he had started to have spells of being awkward when moving from one activity to another in class. He also started to become almost obsessionally interested in his current project work about space travel. In Literacy Hour he had become fidgety and inattentive, giggling inappropriately and becoming easily over-excited at the slightest excuse.

Matters might have drifted on unnoticed but for two incidents which happened within days of one another. The first incident involved a woman visiting the classroom. Martin immediately went up to her and started to act in an over-familiar manner. When asked to return to his seat he tried to kiss her cheek before moving away.

The second incident occurred at the end of the mid-morning break time. Somehow he had become over-excited about the rules of a game, becoming over-aroused. With no obvious warning he then started to punch and kick the children nearest to him. The teacher on playground duty afterwards explained that it took a long time to calm him down. In the end Martin was led to a quiet room, away from the other children. This seemed to help and he rejoined the class group for the final period before lunchtime.

Since both incidents were felt to be so unexpected and out of character, combined with Martin's other problems in the classroom (his obsession with space travel was now interfering with his other work), it was thought advisable, after consulting with his parents, to seek the opinion of Martin's GP and the school's EP.

Was Martin bored at school? Did he have problems making (and keeping) friends? Was he finding his schoolwork too difficult? Was he being bullied, or was something physically wrong which no one had considered?

The EP undertook a behavioural analysis to rule out whether a seizure disorder might be the source of Martin's difficulties. His GP also referred Martin for an EEG and to his local paediatrician. The EP worked through the following evaluation procedure (Table 5.1).

Indication of Possible Seizure	Indication of Possible Behaviour Disturbance
Identical behaviour on each occasion he is aroused	Variation in behaviour with circumstances
No obvious precipitating factors	Commonly precipitated by demands on him or need to avoid a situation
Unresponsive to communication and calming strategies	Response to calming, support and removal from stress inducing situation
Investigation Results *Analysis of Behaviour* Bears little or no relation to context. *Does* tend to happen at certain times of day or after a restless night. *Night time video*: shows typical seizure features *EEG*: shows positive inter-ictal features	*Analysis of behaviour* Tends to be contextually related with certain triggers, e.g. a stranger coming into a room unannounced *Video analysis*: no repetitive behaviours or mannerisms *EEG*: negative evidence of abnormal features present

Lists adapted from J. S. Duncan, S. J. M. Sisodya and J. E. Small (Eds) Epilepsy: From Science to Patient. ILAE, 1999.

Table 5.1 Differentiating seizure and behaviour problems

However, in Martin's case, this did not provide a complete answer to the question – what was causing Martin's problems?

A plan was drawn up together with Martin's parents, his class teacher and the EP. They decided to plan their intervention using the method of differentiation outlined in Table 5.1 and Figure 5.1.

Martin's behaviour improved in the playground and while undertaking group work. However, the obsessionality lingered. Now he started to mislay his belongings and could not always remember where he had put his coat that morning. His parents reported that his sleep patterns had worsened and the periods of forgetfulness started to occur at home.

Martin was referred back to the paediatrician who carried out a 24-hour EEG on him as an in-patient. Further psychological tests were undertaken to study certain parts of Martin's brain – in particular attention and memory. He was also referred for an MRI scan to investigate his brain structure. Clinical results indicated that he did have a type of epilepsy

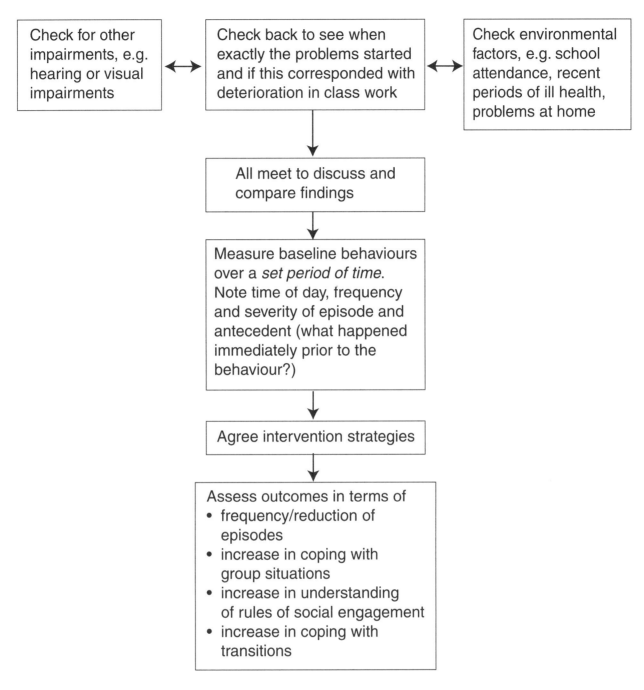

Figure 5.1 Assessment of behaviour problems in epilepsy – basis for intervention

called frontal lobe epilepsy and anti-epileptic medication was prescribed.

Martin's sleep patterns have improved. He is less likely to forget where he is and where his belongings are placed. His attention control has improved and while his behaviour can still be erratic at times, everyone feels that he is easier to live with (including his friends).

There are some instances when epilepsy has an increased

association with behaviour problems and difficulties in learning. Such instances include:

- the frequency and/or severity of the child's seizures;
- the area of the brain from which the excessive activity originates;
- the way in which the 'activity' may then spread;
- actual structural differences, damage or abnormality to a part of the brain which gives rise to both the epilepsy, behaviour problems and also possible associated learning and language difficulties;
- the type of seizure, e.g. a complex partial or simple partial seizure may evolve a series of odd, repetitive behaviours or movements over which the person has no real control; a prolonged absence or series of absences may result in someone completely missing out on an instruction, or misinterpreting it because the crucial words have not been heard, leading to what can appear to the onlooker to be bizarre or insubordinate behaviour.

Medication changes, withdrawal, increase or decrease, or introduction of new drugs can result in behaviour changes. These can be marked if, for example, the child reacts adversely to them. Medication often needs much fine tuning before it is exactly suitable (particularly in adolescence).

Here is a list of other factors you might wish to consider, that may either contribute to a behaviour problem or epilepsy, or both. For further discussion of the multi-factorial nature of behaviour difficulties see Hewett (1998).

Personal factors:

- genetics;
- hormonal imbalance/metabolic disturbance;
- drug reaction/interaction;
- structural brain damage, abnormality or infection;
- other illness – physical or mental;
- pain;
- difficulty with interpersonal relationships – family, peers etc.;
- damage to self or first-hand experience;
- needs and abilities not met – unsatisfactory lifestyle;
- poor sense of self;
- powerlessness – perceived or real.

Environmental factors:
- quality of social life;
- amount and quality of 'space';

- over-protected;
- excessive expectations of others;
- lack of control over environment at various levels;
- perception of events, lifestyle as anxiety provoking.

As can be seen from this far from complete list, there are arguably a number of factors which can contribute to and exacerbate behaviour difficulties. However, some factors can be eliminated through careful investigation of the epilepsy *combined* with behavioural analysis. Therefore, it is important that the support provided to help the child resolve their behaviour difficulties:

- should be focused;
- should follow good practice in collaborative working;
- should maintain a child-centred approach at all times;
- should include parents as partners in order to achieve success in resolution of the situation.

For further reading on this aspect of epilepsy in children we suggest you refer to articles written by David C. Taylor on chronic illnesses in children (www.findarticles.com).

Emerson *et al.* (1994) suggest a range of solutions the teacher, parent, therapist or psychologist may choose from when confronted with a child exhibiting difficult or inappropriate behaviour. The list includes:

- support plans for all concerned;
- task analysis;
- precision (or skill) teaching approaches;
- specific behavioural management;
- incidental teaching strategies;

using the following methods:

- participation indexes;
- logbooks;
- opportunity/goal planning;
- skill teaching;
- ABC charts;
- observation schedules;
- specialised individual programme planning incorporating one or more of the above.

The logging or recording of behavioural episodes in individuals with epilepsy is important. As seen in Martin's case study described earlier, even if there is no obvious activity on the first EEG recording, this does not rule out the hidden presence of an undiagnosed provocateur of the behaviour of interest. Evidence of the teacher, therapist or parents' observations need to be collected carefully and methodically, as they are often pivotal to the making of an unequivocal diagnosis. If a clear-cut relationship is established between an organic cause of the epilepsy and the behaviour (as in some temporal lobe epilepsies), different treatment methods may have to be adopted including:

- adjustment or change of anti-epileptic medication;
- introduction of 'second line' drugs specifically aimed at damping down the individual's tendency to become over-aroused;
- organising environmental safeguards to lessen the risk of over-arousal occurring.

Prevention of over-arousal can be carried out in one or more of the following ways.

1. Show you are not unduly upset or angry about the situation or incident. This can be demonstrated through your own body language, stance, facial expression, tone of voice, distance from the individual 'of concern'. Stand (or sit) slightly to one side of them – so avoiding a confrontational appearance.
2. Be aware of how the child or young person might perceive (or misperceive) what you are saying or doing. Keep what you are saying short, to the point and neutral in tone. Keep your hand gestures 'open'.
3. Know what roles each person will play if a situation develops where over-arousal need to be managed. Make sure *everyone* involved is using the *same* agreed guidelines.
4. Adjust your approach as the incident dictates. Try and appreciate how the child or young person is viewing what is happening. They may be frightened and confused too!
5. Learn from yours and others' experiences. A de-briefing session is valuable for all. It helps you to learn what worked well and what may be improved by a modified method of approach, should a similar incident be repeated.
6. As Hewett (1998) states: 'don't expect to manage all incidents successfully'.

While there is no guaranteed solution to this aspect of the child's behaviour, such approaches have been shown to work effectively. Emblem *et al*. (1998) ascertain that within this approach the child's environment is one that actively fosters acceptable behaviour, where the message being sent out is 'I approve of you as a person but I don't approve of what you are doing.'

The environment also needs to be structured. This does not merely require the setting up of a timetable (and keeping to it), but also the development of a context in which the roles of the people around the child are clear, unambiguous, predictable, i.e. well defined and confident in the execution of their responsibilities within that given context.

Emblem *et al.* insist that the context or environment should be busy without being over-arousing, fun without being out of hand, where children are allowed time and space to be quiet, independent of adult interference, allowed meaningful choices and given respect and acknowledgement for their decisions. Such contexts do not happen by themselves. Like the well-ordered and busy classroom, the informed assessment session, the uneventful family meal – all need to be underpinned by a set of rules and boundaries that need to be consistently adhered to if the status quo is to be maintained. Another method you may wish to consider of controlling the environment is to eliminate the triggers of the inappropriate behaviour. Hewett (1998) provides excellent advice on what he terms 'incident management', i.e. 'a period of time when a person is being very difficult to be with', when a person may be experiencing a possibly prolonged period of over-arousal or when the child presents with a series of behaviours which, while not challenging, may not be appropriate to the context in which they occur.

There are various answers to the questions 'How do I deal with the behaviour when it gets to this stage?' and 'How will I recognise the trigger of the behaviour in the first place?' It is not our intention to offer specific advice on behaviour management, however, you should consider such incidents and their management with an added dimension when working with the child or young person with epilepsy, since as stated earlier, the behaviour may not necessarily be a learned response to a given situation. There may be an underlying physical cause, related both to the child's epilepsy, its cause, treatment, management and the psychosocial consequences of the condition itself.

Summary of management:

- Keep the level of arousal low. Uninhibited or difficult to (self) control behaviour can produce swearing, loud, rude or personally unpleasant comments. Do not take these personally.
- Remain calm and detached from what is happening.

- Plan ahead. Try not to act impulsively even though you may feel that the situation is out of control.
- Try to manage the outcome of the situation so that there are no winners or losers, but an agreed compromise has been reached.
- The incident may result in the child going into a seizure. Be prepared for this eventuality.
- Plan the role each member of staff should play should a difficult situation arise.
- If transitions from one activity or environment to another seem to act as triggers, this can be minimised or avoided by giving the child visual or verbal 'warnings' that such an event is due. This decreases the child's anxiety by reassuring them, making the change in events predictable and understandable.
- Attention control can be problematic when aroused or in a pre-ictal state or when sub-clinical electrical activity may be present in the brain. This needs to be observed and monitored. Keep the focus of attention low key and not taxing. It also helps if the classroom or workspace is kept as structured and free of distractions as possible at such times.

Remember, epilepsy and/or its underlying causes can provoke various types of behaviour. Such problems can occur because:

- Seizures themselves can tire and irritate a child. This is particularly so if they have other difficulties with which to deal.
- Someone who has nocturnal (night-time) seizures will have disturbed sleep patterns.
- Seizures and/or medication may result in impaired awareness of surroundings.
- Seizures can produce inappropriate feelings or auras, e.g. hallucinations, panic attacks, acute feelings of fear, anxiety or anger.
- Frustration can arise because of temporary or progressive loss of skills that can be either physical or cognitive, of which the child may be aware but unable to talk about. (Sometimes called secondary or reactive behavioural difficulties.)
- More severe behavioural disturbance may be a consequence of marked, irreversible loss of language, cognitive and/or motor skills, e.g. as in Landau Kleffner syndrome

(Neville *et al.* 2000).

Management of behaviour problems in this group of individuals is complex and demanding for families, carers and professionals alike. Staff should not be reluctant to seek support and advice from friends and colleagues. More specialised services are available either in the locality, accessed via statutory agencies such as primary care groups, local education offices or social service departments. Learning disability services, clinical psychology, community psychiatry and/or family support services are also invaluable sources of information and specialist help in the form of a behavioural nurse specialist, specialist epilepsy nurse (Sapphire nurse) or cognitive therapist. Such support may take the form of family support and respite care; education and advice on aspects of care and management of the epilepsy itself; treatment compliance; education and training of staff; and advice and implementation of behavioural programmes.

Social aspects

As we noted in earlier chapters, a diagnosis of epilepsy is a life-changing event. It is the process by which the diagnosis is conveyed, what happens afterwards, and the way in which that process alters the parents' constructs about what being well and being ill means that is crucial.

Normally the process of being well is characterised by *not* feeling. If everything is working well, we are not conscious of our bodies functioning – we just know that we are engaging easily with the world around us. This is not the case when we are ill – we become acutely aware of certain parts of our bodies or have a general feeling that engaging with the world takes greater effort. In this instance we consult a doctor. The doctor engages in a process of discovering what is 'wrong' – the cause – and then decides what, if anything, can be done about it. There may be checks at a particular department of the hospital, and maybe an operation, but this takes place within a simple, recognisable context. The pain, the department, the cause and the treatment make sense to the patient. The only situation most people encounter in which this is not so is pregnancy, with its need for careful monitoring. It is interesting that a recent report, *First Class Delivery* (Audit Commission 1997) which focused on ante-natal screening and maternity services in some depth, has come up with findings very similar to those found in Johnson and Thomson's study.

First Class Delivery suggests that some women have poor experiences (either clinically or in their personal care) and their recollection of this remains for many years, affecting their sense of themselves, their recollection of the experience and their attitude to future pregnancies. This is also a theme that emerged from Johnson and Thomson's study. Parents and their children who felt that they had poor experiences remember them in great detail – in some cases for many years. Many of the comments made by these parents suggest that their sense of self was affected, as well as their feelings towards similar future experiences. Epilepsy is in some ways the same, but in others different because in many instances it is more or less permanent. In its chronicity, it is more like problems that affect older adults or those who are HIV positive. Its symptoms can be controlled to a greater or lesser extent but only if a specific regime is followed. It also affects your view of yourself and what others will think of you. It does affect what some people will think of you. It is therefore important that all those with responsibility for the child's development recognise this element in their work with people living with epilepsy.

Initial thoughts about how their epilepsy would affect them could be quite different in individual children. For some, given the reassurance of their parents they seemed to cope:

> She does mention it. But she handles, handles it very well, I think. And she, oh, the first thing she always says when she's had a fit, the first thing she says is 'I'm all right, Mum, I'm all right.' She's really grown-up about it.

> David was never upset by it. Once we'd explained what it was, I think he quite enjoyed it at one time, getting all the fuss.

Others had initial or slight ongoing difficulties:

> At first he was frightened, because he didn't really understand what it meant, you know, he probably thought, you know, 'what's going to happen to me?' He said 'is it something with my brain, or –'. You know, he even asked 'Am I going to die?' And I was just told 'Don't worry, it's just a minor thing.' I told him that his brain stops working for a couple of seconds, and then it starts up again, and now he accepts it.
> Every so often she had a little sort of attack of 'why me' and 'it's not really happening to me', and she 'forgets' to take her tablets.

Others said that they felt that their child was frustrated with the condition, which, as Ford *at al.* (1983), Lechtenberg (1984) and Ziegler (1985) suggest resulted in feelings of loss of control and helplessness:

> Cos I'm still, I'm not allowed to go to many places and it's not fair. Everyone gets to go to the disco. The other day there was a disco, this Friday, and everyone in the whole school went, except me.

Some studies have shown that adjustment difficulties include loss of competence and self-esteem (Matthews *et al.*

1982; Austin *et al.* 1984; Margalit and Heiman 1983; Bjornaes 1988). Comments from parents support this:

> He used to be so fretful, he, I mean, once he'd had an attack he wouldn't go anywhere. He was frightened of going out, he wouldn't go to me mum's, wouldn't go anywhere, school or nothing.

> She only had sort of a close circle of friends, and I think she wanted to be more outgoing, and I think she thought 'Well, nobody's going to like me now I'm epileptic.' In the class it really knocked her self-esteem. It's silly, really.

Self-esteem is developed through everyday reactions between people. There are many interesting theoretical explanations and debates in this area, but they all agree on the one powerful force of how the child believes other people react to them when they behave 'normally'. School, teachers and fellow pupils are of major importance here. Unfortunately, we had reported to us many actions that were less than helpful. If the school reacts defensively with official forms, supervision or rejection of medication, insistence on parents taking their child home if they have had a fit, treating a fit as though it was cardiac arrest, only making the fact of the epilepsy known to a select few as though it was something to be ashamed of – all these will naturally make the child feel very different and excluded.

One vivid example demonstrates this:

> At one stage, he had, er, a woman – when the statement finally come through – there was a nice lady up at the school, and this is what his statement involved, who followed him from lesson to lesson, to make sure he was safe. I can understand that, I suppose it's very helpful, but it just didn't work. He was determined that this woman was not going to follow him round in front of his mates and … wasn't just walking round with the crowd, she was – I think she was actually segregating him and making him walk holding hands. And teenagers do not want to hold hands … he was getting more and more alienated from the lads around him, which was then having this knock-on effect of the bullying and anything else – the mickey-taking, yes, because kids are cruel, they're really, really cruel.

The knowledge that a child has epilepsy has an immediate and significant impact on the family unit as a whole, which may lead to changes in family dynamics. As reported by Lechtenberg (1984) the child who is diagnosed as having epilepsy often becomes the focus of the parents' attention. Parents in this sample confirmed that this can happen:

> But, like, um, when you're out, you tend to watch that one more than the little ones, you know what I mean, whereas you should be watching the little uns, and not the biggest one. But your mind's constantly sort of – 'where is she, she hasn't

wandered off', you know, in case she's had a black-out and things like that. Um, so it's affected us all like that.

Another parent was very aware of the attention that she and her husband paid their son with epilepsy. She employed strategies to ensure that her other son did not feel neglected:

I was concerned because sometimes he would say 'you love Brian more than me', because obviously he has had a lot of attention, but you get that with children anyway. We've always made a thing about David being the eldest, trying to make him special in that way, that he does everything first, before Brian. So we are aware, and we have to be very careful, but I think we've got it right – you don't know until they're older.

Parents also commented on the effect that the practicalities of the condition had on the other children in the family:

But it had a terrible effect on them two, well, you know, because I'd sort of disappear or – overnight, and I'm not there. And they got terribly anxious, you know, they wouldn't let me out of their sight, because they never knew when I was coming back. You know, Karen is poorly and that, so I used to have to sneak off. When – we've only been here six years, and before that, you know, I just used to ring me mum and say 'We're going to the hospital.'

Not only does the condition affect siblings, many of the mothers said that the child's father had difficulties accepting the diagnosis, which sometimes led to denial:

As far as he was concerned it was his child and there was nothing wrong with his children, sort of thing, and he just wouldn't accept it anyway.

Again, this will suggest to the child that there is something to be ashamed of. Implications for family life also extend to the activities that parents felt they could do with their child which obviously has consequences for other children in the family:

Just that it's terrible and it like ruins your life. It ruins our life. That sounds selfish, but it does. You know like, you're wanting to go out somewhere and like, we're all ready, and Tracey has a seizure. So you can't go for like an hour, an hour and half afterwards. And we wanted to take her to watch 'Disney on Ice', but like I said, it's going to sound really bad, but it's a waste of money. If she goes and has a seizure in the middle of it, and we have to come home, what's the point in going?

What parents actually want from their interaction with the medical profession first is reassurance:

You know, that's what you needed, really, just someone to say, you know, this is, like, epilepsy is this, this is what happens, this is, like, the result, you know, you can live a normal life. You – you'd have been – you know, you'd have got – you'd have got on with life better, really, you know.

After the diagnosis of epilepsy is confirmed parents then need clear, simple information about the effects and implications for their child. They also need honesty. They also need to recognise that it is difficult for doctors to know what is realistic to say about the future, particularly in the early stages of the diagnosis (see earlier). As the next comment from a parent demonstrates – it is difficult to make long term predictions of outcome in some instances:

> And they kept telling us that he would grow out of it, because nocturnal epilepsy, they expected him to grow out of it. Well, he's nineteen, he still hasn't, and I don't suppose that he will now. I don't know they give you that false hope, and then it's broken.

Procedures for providing information and supporting families in both hospitals and schools seem to be inconsistent. Information seems to be lost between health and education. At present the procedures that are in place tend to be ineffective because they are purely administrative structures seeking to convey generalised information that does not focus on the effects of the condition on an individual child. In many cases, the school's priority seems to be to safeguard itself against the possibility of any liability rather than help the children. It is in such contexts that the epilepsy liaison nurse can prove to be pivotal in ensuring successful information exchange and transfer.

Therefore, it cannot be stressed enough that the only effective way in which parents and teachers can work together is on an *informal* basis, sharing valuable information without fear of repercussions. If teachers have had no previous experiences, someone with a medical background must validate the epilepsy information held by parents. This person can then take some responsibility for agreeing that the actions proposed by the school are reasonable. As a preference there should be a joint meeting of parents, teachers, the epilepsy liaison nurse and the 'medic' so that everyone can ask questions, express views and concerns and share information.

Chapter 6

Language and Communication Problems Associated with Epilepsy and Related Syndromes

Language and allied cognitive processes in the brain are highly susceptible to interference from a number of causal and associated factors (Rutter 1978; Adams *et al.* 1997) with Robinson (1991) referring to the presence of focal brain lesions as a particular cause for the failure of development of language-related skills. Although little research has been carried out on the association between epilepsy and language disability – with the exception of a few notable studies (Haynes and Naidoo 1991; Robinson 1987; Parkinson 1999) – some work has been carried out investigating the language patterns of children with Landau Kleffner syndrome (Lees 1993; Bishop and Rosenbloom 1987).

Some research has indicated that because the brain demands more glucose and oxygen when epileptic discharges occur, prolonged seizures have an adverse effect on oxygen uptake which can ultimately lead to brain damage. Such damage can vary from subtle problems with the 'fine wiring' needed for language and other higher level processes, e.g. some types of memory, analytical thinking and information processing, through to more global damage resulting in a generalised effect on learning and development.

Lees and Neville (1990) proposed a method of classifying potential causes of a particular epilepsy syndrome, acquired convulsive aphasia, which could be applied to some of the other epilepsy-associated disorders where loss of already acquired language was a feature. They proposed that such types of language disability could be caused by:

- Prolonged convulsive status (also known as status epilepticus).
- A post-ictal phenomenon (sometimes seen as a temporary loss of speech, lack of comprehension or mild paralysis of some of the muscles on one side of the face).
- A primary pathology, e.g. a cerebral infection such as meningitis, or temporal lobe disease.
- A feature of non-convulsive status (which could be temporary).
- A psychological reaction to epilepsy, e.g. selective mutism.
- An organic event occurring with epilepsy but not covered above.

Other factors could be added to this list such as the results of head injury, effects of prolonged or high levels of medication, post-epilepsy surgery, or late onset epilepsies of childhood.

It is not the remit of this book to provide the reader with a guide to the causes of epilepsy in any detail. Neither is this chapter a definitive guide to the diagnosis and differentiation of language disability subtypes. However, there are certain aspects of a child's epilepsy that might lead the teacher, parent, carer or professional involved to consider whether they have an undiagnosed language impairment. Such an impairment might adversely affect the child's learning, social interaction, academic performance, behaviour and general quality of life if undiagnosed or not taken account of when planning future support needs and curriculum access.

So, what do we need to consider when exploring the possibility of the presence of a language impairment in the child with epilepsy?

Epilepsy-related factors

It is important to find out as precisely as possible when the epilepsy started. This is an essential point of information to establish, when diagnosing the type of language disability present.

Generally speaking, if there has been a period (or apparent period) of normal language and cognitive development prior to the onset of epilepsy, the prognosis for language development is likely to be more optimistic. If the child has been able to acquire the early elements and rules of language and communication, i.e. the foundations of language, then the prospects for subsequent language development are brighter. However, in some instances there is a risk that the pattern of learning higher level language and information processing may be disordered, i.e. uneven in its profile of acquisition (see later).

If the epilepsy is due to an underlying brain abnormality that was caused in the early stages of foetal development, then regardless of the time at which epilepsy first makes its presence known, the child will be at much greater risk of more complex language and cognitive difficulties. Indeed this can be one of the reasons why children with the more complex epilepsies of childhood can appear to experience both delayed and disordered language development.

Types of seizures and language disability

Research carried out by Parkinson (1999) found that in a sample of 109 children with complex (hard to manage) or treatment-resistant epilepsies, those with predominantly generalised seizure disorders were more likely to be language delayed. Children with partial seizures had an increased likelihood of developing high level language and or pragmatic disorders (depending on the location of the epileptic focus). While this research is in no way conclusive, it does alert all those involved with children who have more difficult epilepsies to the likelihood of certain language problems being associated with particular types of seizure disorder.

Children with complex partial seizures with frontal lobe onset, which then develop secondary generalisation into tonic-clonic seizures, are therefore likely to have mixed language profiles with elements of delay and disorder. If the epilepsy onset was early then the language delay will probably be predominant. Children with frontal lobe epilepsy syndromes will also be at increased risk of information processing, memory and social use of language (pragmatic) difficulties. Such difficulties may manifest themselves as behaviour or idiosyncratic personality problems, e.g. a tendency to rigid thinking, obsessionality and/or an inability to cope with transitions. Understanding of the subtleties of language such as negotiation and rules of social interaction can be impaired. Children with temporal lobe epilepsy or predominantly temporal lobe-oriented seizures are, if the dominant temporal lobe is affected, those most at risk of impaired language – both in terms of understanding what is said to them or how they process the information and reassemble their replies. Someone with a problem originating from the outer side of the (usually left) temporal lobe may have difficulties with speech (expressive language) that manifest as:

- word searching and finding difficulties;

- knowing the target word but unable to say it;
- using many words (circumlocution) to describe the target word;
- repeating a word used earlier which *sounds* like the target word or has a similar *meaning*;
- an ability to string words together but temporarily unable to speak clearly.

Such problems can occur after partial seizures involving a temporal lobe focus (focal- or localisation-related seizures). Such problems are important to note both for the purposes of putting a support plan in place, and particularly for the paediatrician or paediatric neurologist. This type of information helps to establish both the *area* of the brain from which the epilepsy is generated, and how far the distributed effect may extend and impinge on other brain functions.

There is no directly comparable localisation of function in the right (non-dominant) hemisphere. However, some children have experienced difficulties in the following:

- recognising and repeating musical notes;
- picking out a tune;
- singing in tune;
- reduced intonation pattern when speaking, e.g. voice can sound monotonous in older children and young people;
- inappropriate or over-literal sense of humour;
- poor grasp of irony;
- little or no understanding of idioms or metaphors;
- poor comprehension of colloquial speech or slang;
- little or no appreciation of implied meaning.

Children with frontal lobe seizures have symptoms that are less well defined (see p. viii and 84). Because there are so many connecting fibres that carry electrical impulses (and messages) to and from the frontal lobes and the temporal lobes, it is often difficult to ascertain precisely exactly where the epileptic focus is sited. As well as influencing memory, personality alertness, attention control, control of anxiety and fear, the frontal lobes also seem to control the *initiation* and *coordination* of certain groups of muscles. Therefore some children may not merely experience difficulties in finding a word but have problems initiating the movements required to make (and sequence) the requisite sounds. This condition is sometimes called verbal dyspraxia. The muscle groups are unimpaired but the programming of their initiation and coordination can be impaired either during or following a seizure.

Certain categories and aspects of language seem to be more

susceptible to damage or failure to acquire in children with epilepsy who are language disordered. These include:

- reversible passive verbs, e.g. the girl is chasing the boy;
- post-modified subject, e.g. the man pushing the lorry is muddy;
- relative clauses, e.g. the book is on the shelf that is crooked.

It seems that children in this group have difficulty carrying out requests correctly when word order and sequencing of information is necessary. This difficulty may become more pronounced as larger and increasingly complex information assimilation is demanded. Information of 'low imageability', i.e. that is difficult to visualise, or which has few or no contextual clues, may also present problems when delivered verbally. If in doubt the teacher, psychologist or therapist is advised, whenever possible, to support with visual reinforcement, either in the form of notes or synopses.

It is recognised in the literature that there is a heightened incidence of poor attention control, auditory memory and recall of words and phonemic units in children with epilepsy. Such processes are not just prone to interruption from overt seizures, but also from inter-ictal electrical activity within the child's brain, i.e. at the level of neuro-transmission and brain metabolism. Gallassi *et al.* (1988) found that memory impairment occurred in children following seizure disturbance, particularly in association with complex partial seizures. Brown (1990) has reported inter-ictal cognitive changes associated with processing of verbal language. This feature was more pronounced in new learning and retention of material.

Medication effect

Appleton (1995) admitted that while the more recently introduced anti-epileptic drugs (AEDs) have a more acceptable safety record regarding side effects, there is still a relative lack of understanding concerning the potential for the more discrete side effects of drugs on such areas as vigilance, attention control, cognition and language function. Inevitably a balance has to be struck between seizure management and control and drug effect. Even when examining the evidence for the presence or absence of a particular feature (or effect) it cannot necessarily be ascertained whether:

a) the features observed are a direct drug effect;

b) the features observed are a result of inter-drug synergic effect;

c) in the case of newly diagnosed epilepsy, the child is still in a state of transition;

d) there is drug acclimatisation;

e) there is drug tolerance;

f) the seizures themselves (and/or the underlying cause of those seizures) are exerting a compounding effect on intellectual functioning and language competence.

There is no simple answer to the question 'Is the problem caused by/made worse by, medication effect?' in the same way that we cannot always state that what we are observing is seizure effect. Only by a process of careful observation and accurate record-keeping can we ensure the child is being given the best possible chance to experience a more than acceptable quality of life and opportunity.

Walker and Shorvon (1999) note the following potential side effects (usually dose-related) that might have a bearing on a child's academic performance in language, learning and social skills:

- Unsteadiness
- Fatigue
- Headache
- Stomach upset
- General slowness

(Note: with the constant changes and advances in medicine and introduction of new drugs, the information in this section while correct at the time of going to press will soon become out of date. For further information refer to the BEA website, the National Society for Epilepsy (see Useful Addresses/Internet Sites) or the prescribing physician.)

Seizure frequency and duration

Prolonged seizures of any type are not satisfactory. Seizures involving loss of consciousness which are prolonged or which cluster without the person regaining consciousness between one and the next can be detrimental to brain function. Language and the higher thought and associated cognitive processes are vulnerable to damage when situations involving prolonged seizure activity arise. The effect on language function, because it draws on a number of centres in the brain, tends to be global. Because language and cognition are inextricably linked, there is often a corresponding effect on intellectual functioning which can result in a transient, or more long-term loss of skills. Assessment and reassessment of children or young people who have encountered these episodes is therefore important. Compensating for and re-teaching lost skills in order for the child to continue to develop and progress is vital and should be planned for at the earliest opportunity.

Language and communication problems associated with epilepsy syndromes (or associated syndromes where epilepsy is a major feature)

In 30–40 per cent of children with epilepsy, it may not be possible to identify an epilepsy syndrome because the symptoms with which the child presents do not quite fit the criteria for assigning certain syndromic diagnoses. However, there are syndromes that have language disability as a recognised component. Until comparatively recently, many epilepsy textbooks and journals did not refer to the presence of any kind of language or communication problems. Occasionally there might have been reference to mental slowing, attention difficulties or memory problems. There is a growing trend now to describe the features or characteristics of a syndrome in more holistic terms. This view of the whole child and how they interact with the world is a reflection of the broader view now being taken by medical practitioners and allied professions – a view which is to be encouraged.

The following epilepsies and epilepsy-related syndromes all have associated language and communication (which may include speech) problems, of varying degrees of severity. Many also have learning difficulties associated with them. The learning problems may be specific, uneven or generalised (global), depending on the age of onset and presence or absence of other neurological difficulties.

Benign rolandic epilepsy (also known as benign partial epilepsy with centro-temporal (rolandic) spikes)

Age of onset: 4–10 years (peak 7–9 years)
Prevalence: most common partial epilepsy of childhood. Accounts for 10–15% of all childhood epilepsies.
Problems:

- disturbance in processing auditory information;
- lack of coordination of lips, tongue and teeth for eating and speech which may be transient;
- verbal memory not as good as visual memory.

West syndrome and hypsarrhythmia/infantile spasms

Age of onset: 2–12 months (peak 5–9 months)
Prevalence: rare, 1–5% of childhood epilepsy
Problems:
- global learning difficulties (60–70%);
- language delay (60%);

Note: 50–60% go on to develop Lennox-Gastaut syndrome. Psychomotor development often appears to stop after onset. Hypsarrhythmia is the name given to the appearance of the EEG between 'spikes'.

Lennox-Gastaut syndrome

Age of onset: 1–8 years (peak 3–5 years)
Prevalence: uncommon, 1–5% of all childhood epilepsy
Problems:
- moderate to severe development delay;
- language delay with occasional disordered components. Sometimes first words may be acquired then subsequently lost. Some improvement has been noted in verbal communication in late adolescence and as seizures reduce;
- attention problems;
- pragmatic difficulties;
- may have poor palatal, pharyngeal and oro-motor problems affecting eating and swallowing in the early years.

Note: 20% have a history of West's syndrome. Difficult behaviour can mask communication difficulties in some children. Some children may appear to have a brief window of normal development before onset. Cryptogenic cases, i.e. those for which a cause is suspected but not confirmed, tend to have a better outlook than symptomatic cases, i.e. those for whom seizures are indicators of an underlying brain pathology or disease.

Continuous spike-waves during slow-wave sleep or CSWS (Electrical Status in Slow Wave Sleep, ESES) (see also Landau Kleffner syndrome)

Onset: 8 months to 12 years (peak 7–12 years)
Prevalence: rare
Problems:

- developmental delay – often after a period of normal development of several years;
- language and cognitive loss (plus hemiplegia) prior to seizure onset;
- behaviour and attention difficulties – can present as similar to attention deficit hyperactivity disorder (ADHD) or attention deficit disorder (ADD) in the early stages prior to seizure onset (20%).

This condition often occurs in a child with a pre-existing epilepsy where the seizures appear well controlled. Often manifests as behavioural change and cognitive deterioration without obvious seizures. Needs nocturnal EEG for diagnosis. About 50% regain early language skills as seizures diminish in early to mid-adolescence.

Rasmussen's syndrome

Onset: 14 months to 14 years
Prevalence: rare
Problems:
- cognitive decline after a period of normal development;
- dysarthria (poor articulation of speech sounds);
- verbal/oral dyspraxia (poor motor programming for initiation and sequencing of speech sounds and/or movements for eating, chewing and swallowing);
- hemiplegia in later stages.
- epilepsy partialis continua (periods of difficult to control one-sided twitching)

Note: this condition is characterised by atrophy of the brain on the affected side which may be treated by surgery (hemispherectomy), after which children may become seizure-free. Cognition and language may improve even if the dominant hemisphere containing the main language centres is removed, particularly if surgery is carried out early.

Landau-Kleffner syndrome (see also ESES)

Acquired epileptic aphasia
Acquired convulsive aphasia
Age of onset: 2–10 years (peak 5–7 years)
Prevalence: rare

Problems:

- loss of language comprehension after a period of normal development (can appear to be profoundly deaf or suffer from an inability to remember the meaning of sound (auditory agnosia));
- diminished expressive language which can revert to idiosyncratic or stereotyped phrases, jargon which may or may not be accompanied by odd intonation;
- loss of social communication;
- some children may have mild developmental problems prior to the period of sudden loss of skills but later regress (in excess of that commonly seen in autism) (Neville *et al.* 2000);
- behaviour problems may be severe;
- secondary reactive behavioural problems to the condition itself;
- stereotyped, ritualised, repetitive play;
- characteristics of ADD or ADHD.

Note: some cases may be diagnosed as pervasive developmental disorder not otherwise specified or atypical autism (PDDNOS: DSM-IV.APA, 1994). Such cases are normally only found in child development centres, specialist school provision for language-impaired children or language units; the latter usually for assessment purposes. Some children may have EEG abnormalities but no seizures. See case study described by Vance (1991) for further discussion of educational and therapeutic implications.

Other special conditions associated with epilepsy which may have language disability and cognitive impairment include:

- *Tuberous sclerosis.* May have delayed language development in line with learning disability.
- *Neurofibromatosis.* Similar to above but may be complicated by other neurological problems.
- *Down's syndrome* (6–8% with epilepsy). Learning disability, language delay, hearing impairment and facial hypotonia can all affect the communication abilities of children with Down's syndrome. Pre-ictal phenomena and inter-ictal electrical discharges can adversely affect learning and attention control. AEDs can also exacerbate task orientation, learning and skill retention, particularly when the child has moved on to more abstract learning of language concepts.
- *Rett syndrome* (> 90% have epilepsy). Most of the girls with this syndrome (70–80%) have epilepsy, with onset of seizures at the ages of between three and five years. Many react adversely to medication regimes (Brodtkorb 1999).

Language delay is global in all cases and can be severe to profound.

- *Fragile X syndrome* (20–40% have epilepsy). Learning disability and language delay is generally in the mild to moderate range. However, social anxiety and avoidance of eye contact and poor concentration can contribute to a disordered profile of language acquisition, particularly social and abstract components of language. Some children may fulfil some of the criteria for autistic spectrum disorder when young and ADHD throughout childhood and adolescence (Hagerman *et al.* 1989).
- *Angelman's syndrome* (> 80% develop epilepsy). Known association with severe learning disability and global language delay accompanied by inappropriate smiling and laughter. Expressive language is much more impaired than receptive abilities. Social use of language is poor with children exhibiting some behavioural features in common with autistic spectrum disorder (Steffenberg *et al.* 1996).

Note: There is an acknowledged association in the literature between epilepsy and autism/autistic spectrum disorder with learning disability (up to 50% of affected cases).

Management issues and principles

Many of the points made in this section will seem obvious and a matter of common sense. Yet as we have observed, teachers, carers, therapists and '-ologists' disregard the guidelines for good practice which should be second nature to us all.

General principles of management and support of children with language disability and epilepsy

We need to

1. Understand the exact nature of the language impairment.
2. Make sure others understand the type and nature of the difficulties the child has in
   a) understanding what is said
   b) processing that information   – sorting it out
       – remembering it
       – recalling it at a suitable time and place
       – reassembling the information into a verbal (or written) form
   c) expressing a response

    d) adhering to the rules of social engagement, e.g. contextual appropriateness, topic management, relevance.
3. Ensure that the child remains central to the planning and support required at classroom, whole school and community levels.
4. Ensure support is available at resource, policy and implementation levels.
5. Monitor and review the child's progress through
    a) standard school/class/individual evaluation systems
    b) record-keeping of   – changes in medication/ treatment
                     – seizure type, frequency and times of episodes/ events
                     – changes in academic performance, alertness, behaviour, attention, mood
                     – assessment and reassessment of language competency and related cognitive abilities.
6. Ensure formal assessments are carried out at a time of day when the child is likely to be at their best.
7. Parents and primary carers are partners and support systems should reflect and enhance that partnership, e.g. accurate and up-to-date maintenance of home–school diaries and seizure logbooks.
8. Don't expect to manage everything successfully.
9. Know who to call on if you are concerned about a change in the child's performance, particularly if you suspect a plateauing or loss of skills.

When organising information delivery within a class or other setting, you may find it helpful to bear the following in mind.

- Keep information delivery short and to the point. If necessary break it down into small chunks.
- Information containing abstract or unorthodox concepts may be unexpectedly difficult to assimilate if not reinforced by visual prompts and contextual cues.
- Explain what you are going to do and want the child to do as simply as possible. Check the child has understood. This is particularly important if it is an instruction in a practical lesson or where safety might be an issue, especially if the child is known to experience absence seizures.
- If you are testing/assessing you may have to allow for a question to be repeated even though under normal circumstances this option would not usually be permitted.

- Remember that children with epilepsy may have subtle, unusual and possibly mixed types of language problems that demand different types of approach assessment and remediation that may need additional provision of space and time.
- Teamwork is vital if the child is to be supported effectively.

Services at primary level (school, GP, epilepsy liaison nurse, social services, speech and language therapy and child psychology (educational psychology)), will need to have an established link with more specialised (possibly hospital, child development or specialist clinical) services with clear information exchange, reassessment and service access. The child's language disability is probably linked to other problems, e.g. behaviour, cognitive, general health, other neurologically-related difficulties, all of which need varying amounts of support and intervention throughout the child's education. The nature, pattern and severity of seizures and degree of capacity imposed by the epilepsy and its treatment will vary during the child's life, e.g. at onset of puberty. Services will need to maintain an essentially flexible, child-centred approach if the child's needs are to be met.

Chapter 7

Quality of Life

As we have seen from the subjects covered in the earlier chapters of this book, epilepsy is not simply a medical problem – it can be a family problem, a social, educational and possibly an employment issue. Like it or not, people with epilepsy are inevitably affected by the views and attitudes held by society. We hope that this book has demonstrated that epilepsy represents a group of symptoms that can vary greatly from one person to another. It has many underlying causes and its impact on people's lives can range from the inconvenient to the catastrophic. This is why it is important not to label a person as 'an epileptic' because this encourages us to think of people with epilepsy in a stereotyped way – which is, as we have seen, clearly not the case. Also, the use of such a label tends to focus on the epilepsy and not the person, when in fact the emphasis should be in reverse. This is important if we are to ensure that children and young people achieve an optimum quality of life without the pressure and possible prejudice that such a label may engender.

What do we mean by optimum 'quality of life'? We view quality of life as a marker of an individual's well-being in their day-to-day life. Although a subjective term, several measures of it exist (especially in connection with health-oriented research into evidence-based medicine). Professionals in social, educational or primarily therapeutic domains will each define it from a slightly different standpoint. However, the view is essentially 'person-centred' and in this instance refers to a child or young person living with epilepsy.

Epilepsy surveys of quality of life

In 1994 the Epilepsy Task Force devised a 30-item questionnaire that was sent to children with epilepsy whose families were members of the BEA. Free text comments were made by over 400 of the 896 people who responded within the first two weeks. The survey, entitled *The Childhood Epilepsy Survey – Making Waves* (reported on in Brown 1994) was the first of a series of recent attempts to analyse the effects of epilepsy on children and their families in real life rather than in the laboratory. Information was sought on seizures, medication, and attitudes towards seizures, mediation and communication with doctors and the perceived effects of epilepsy on activities, relationships, school life and personal self-esteem. One free text entry (cited in Brown 1994) read:

> I feel very tired at school. I feel I should be able to concentrate better. This makes me want to stop taking the tablets.

And another,

> I want my epilepsy to go, it's hard to do school work. I feel tired a lot, and forgetful, and writing legibly is difficult.

One child wrote,

> I feel separate and different than other people and I feel a lot less cleverer than other people.

A sobering comment came from one questionnaire,

> It isn't fair how people discriminate against individuals who unfortunately have epilepsy, especially teachers. I think they should be made more aware of the condition and also later on in life so should employers.

Two subsequent surveys were carried out in 1995, *Positive Action for Better Services* (Collings 1995) and 2000 (*Charter 2000 Survey*) for the BEA. Although only 10.2 per cent of respondents were under 16 years of age in the 1995 survey and 16 per cent in full-time education in the 2000 survey, the results are nevertheless of interest.

Side effects of medication as an issue seems to have increased in importance over the period the surveys were undertaken, with 83.6 per cent of the 971 respondents from *Charter 2000* experiencing problems of varying severity. More than 50 per cent encountered problems with access to or encounters with GPs and neurologists/epilepsy specialists in marked contrast to the 1995 survey. However, since the majority of respondents were (a) adults and (b) as Collings describes, a group which may reflect an increasing awareness of and knowledge of treatment issues (with a more general more consumer-oriented culture), these views should be accepted with a certain degree of caution.

Problems experienced by children and young people with epilepsy relating to school and further education appeared to fall slightly between 1995 and the 2000 survey.

Over the 10-year period from 1990 to 2000, Collings felt that the results showed little change either way in terms of the impact of epilepsy on social life, leisure activities, self-image, personal relationships and society's attitudes, vocational training and having a family. All or some of these aspects of quality of life presented problems of varying severity to between 44 and 65 per cent of respondents.

Factors which featured significantly as associated with experiencing problems with well-being were:

- overall epilepsy management;
- obtaining the right treatment;
- leading an active social life;
- personal relationships.

Lower levels of well-being were associated, unsurprisingly, with:

- high seizure frequency;
- younger people;
- earlier age of onset of epilepsy.

One respondent, quoted in the BEA report *Agenda for Action: Epilepsy in the New Millennium* (BEA 2000) wrote,

> People often put me down because of my epilepsy. They think I am stupid or incapable of doing anything. I don't like their attitude. I'm tired of being left out, passed over, and ignored because of my epilepsy.

Ensuring good quality of life requires an approach that involves three different frames of reference.

1. *Child-centred*. This approach looks at personal attributes, i.e., how they feel about themselves as individuals, about their epilepsy and their environment, their ability, the nature and management of their epilepsy and their history, i.e. how the child arrived at this point in time and the effect of significant events en route.
2. *Changes that have taken place compared with how life is now.* For instance, what form does the treatment of the epilepsy now take? How much does this intrude on daily life? Has the type or frequency of the seizure changed and how

does this impinge on current lifestyle? Other areas looked at in this section might include independence, social interaction, behaviour, community participation and peer contact, and whether the family's or carers' views have changed over the months or years.

3. *The effect of epilepsy on the people around the individual concerned.* Normally, effect on parents and carers is the main area of interest here, but could be extended easily to include teachers, support workers and the child's friends.

Children with epilepsy can be unintentionally devalued both by society and denied access to what Wolfensberger *et al.* (1996) call 'the good things in life'. They include:

- a family or small group home including friends of their choice;
- a place to call home;
- a social group including friends;
- opportunities and experiences to discover and develop skills, abilities and talents;
- to be treated with respect;
- to be treated honestly;
- to be treated justly;
- to be treated as an individual in one's own right (not treated as a label);
- given access to facilities to which we are all entitled to use and visit including social facilities;
- being able to make a contribution and having that recognised and valued;
- not to be pre-judged or patronised.

As previously stated, epilepsy is a chronic condition – it changes over time and its unpredictability is hard to cope with for the individual and difficult to plan for *because* of the very nature of that unpredictability. However, in our efforts to plan for this unpredictability, it is easy to lose sight of the fact that for most of the time, most children with epilepsy lead reasonably normal lives. Only when epileptic seizures become out of control or a child goes into status epilepticus, does the perspective change – much like when any child becomes acutely ill or needs emergency treatment. What such episodes must not do is dictate how the child's life should then be prescribed. Obviously, this last statement is an over-generalisation since children's epilepsies can vary on a spectrum between the benign epilepsies of childhood and epilepsies that are symptomatic of degenerative conditions, or associated with other complex neurological impairments. Nevertheless, the governing underlying principle should remain the same, i.e. that quality of life should be fought for, maintained and encouraged as much as and wherever possible.

We can support this endeavour in ways that have been described in the preceding chapters of this book. Attendance at mainstream school should be one of *the* primary goals, for example. In a minority of instances where children have very complex, life threatening or intractable (resistant to treatment) epilepsy, in association with learning difficulties, severe behavioural or psychiatric difficulties and/or cerebral palsy, or require high levels (e.g. 24-hour) of medical care, more specialist (possibly residential) provision may be considered. Even if specialist schooling is required, this should not in any way deprive the child of any of the good things in life listed earlier.

Research studies show that despite attending mainstream or highly supported school placements, many children with epilepsy continue to underachieve. As discussed earlier, there is a variety of reasons for this. Epilepsy itself and the effect of AEDs can, as we have seen, impair aspects of learning and retention of information. Many children with epilepsy are almost *expected* not to perform as well as their peers, so that this expectation of underachievement by parents, teachers and other professionals can become a self-fulfilling prophecy. The social implications of epilepsy, interrupted schooling, feelings of poor self-worth, insecurities, anxieties and frustration about the school experience, can all contribute to underachievement (Walker and Shorvon 1999).

The literature mentions parental over-anxiety and the tendency for over-vigilance and over-protectiveness of their children. Two further points should be borne in mind. First, professionals can lose sight of what the parents may have gone through emotionally and psychologically before they come into contact with them. Many parents will have experienced emotional roller-coaster rides with the child's health, access to and treatment by a bewildering variety of services, and very steep learning curves on subjects from education rules and regulations to Benefits Agency and National Health Service budgets/resources for specialist hospital and allied services. Secondly, the professionals themselves can feel unsupported and lacking in knowledge, particularly when confronted with a child who has one of the more unusual epilepsy syndromes. Professionals should not be afraid to admit their uncertainties to parents and colleagues. It is widely recognised that parents are an often overlooked but invaluable source of information to professionals involved in assessment and education of their child.

What factors should we look for when considering whether a child's quality of life should contain more 'good things'? The following are considered to have a significant bearing:

- over-protection;
- over-vigilance;
- over-indulgence of behaviour normally regarded as inappropriate or unacceptable;
- the child's own self-perception and level of self-esteem;
- attitudes of others (siblings, friends, relatives etc.) (a) to the child and (b) to the epilepsy;
- self-expectation and expectation of others;
- access (a) personally, (b) socially, (c) academically, and (d) post-school (careers, higher education, further education, meaningful employment).

Protection is something we all do when children are young and when we feel they are vulnerable to unpleasant external influences that might put them at risk of self-harm or harm from others. Children who experience seizures which are unpredictable in time and frequency of onset, when seizures are not preceded by a warning aura or pre-ictal period of some kind (e.g. headache or disturbed sleep), are likely to place themselves in a context of higher risk of self-injury (especially in atonic seizures or drop attacks) than other children with well-controlled seizures or seizures which only occur at night. Therefore, the instinct to protect your child, or the child in your care, tends to be over-magnified as the risk – perceived or otherwise – increases.

Risk Management

While the danger can never be removed completely it can be reduced significantly through the use of risk management. Such a rationale lessens both the child's anxiety (because they know the situation is under control) and the adult's concern (because they have systems in place to cope with such an eventuality if and/or when it arises). Quality of life can be seriously diminished for parents, child, siblings and peers if space and time is not built into the child's lifestyle so that serious risk is *minimised* and *controlled* while still allowing the child to learn to live with the day-to-day risks that we all must learn to cope with. 'Growing up requires risks to achieve benefits' (Freeman *et al.* 1997), and the child with epilepsy needs such opportunities in order to lead an independent and fulfilling life.

A child for whom the epilepsy has been used as an excuse for their behaviour or way of gaining special treatment on the pretext that they have 'suffered' so much can also be deprived of a good quality of life. They are no longer able to form or maintain social relationships, visit places that require certain codes of conduct, share activities with friends and family which demand cooperation and adherence to certain (even simple) rules of social engagement. Sometimes, when the epilepsy is controlled, the underlying causes defined and, where possible, treated, the legacy of over-indulgence remains. In order to help such children and their families, one needs to work with and support the family as a whole. This is important as over-indulgence – conscious or otherwise – can occur for many reasons that need to be worked through before the child *and* the family can move forward.

Self-esteem and self-worth can adversely affect many individuals. Indeed there is a recognised risk of adolescents developing depressive or anxiety-related illnesses as a reaction to or as a secondary development of their epilepsy. Accepting a diagnosis of epilepsy is very hard both for the child and the family. The news can be devastating, particularly if the child is recovering well from an acute illness, injury or surgery, only to be told that they have epilepsy too. People react differently, but for the individual child or young person on the threshold of life, the news can be a great blow. Anger, shock and frustration at the imposed changes to their lives, knowledge that skills may have been lost and an overwhelming feeling of failure and injustice, can compound an already difficult situation.

However, there are people and services (see Useful Addresses/Internet Sites) that can help. Some of these will have direct experience of supporting people through the difficult early stages of confirmation of diagnosis, acceptance and adjustment. Some of the specialist epilepsy charities run helplines, websites, regional and district meetings and self-help groups. These can be an invaluable source of help and support. They are arenas where you can meet specialists and others with epilepsy to compare notes and ask questions you might feel unable to voice in a more formal setting.

In an educational or therapeutic setting, low self-esteem and feelings of poor self-worth can be demonstrated when the individual shows some of the following:

- lethargy;
- irritability for no apparent reason;
- irrational mood swings;
- social withdrawal;
- non-submission of coursework or homework which is spasmodic or unexpected;
- evasiveness;
- absconds;
- emotional, e.g. cries easily;
- prone to anger and intolerance of others.

Specialist clinical psychology (hospital and community based) services together with counselling (GP or hospital based) can significantly improve the outlook of individuals finding it difficult to come to terms with or adjusting to changes in the nature of their epilepsy.

A vulnerable point in the life of a young person is when they have to consider post-school provision or a move into employment. They can be faced with restrictions in lifestyle choices that can directly impinge on their quality of life. Such restrictions in employment opportunities, although small, can add to an adolescent's frustration, anger over their epilepsy and feelings of isolation and 'why me?' Such feelings can have a detrimental effect on the individual's natural striving to achieve independence. Family, school, psychology and GP services all have important roles to play in encouraging and supporting the young person to develop feelings of self-worth and self-belief in the right to achieve as complete and fulfilling a life as possible.

Quality of life, learning disability and epilepsy

For many children and young people with epilepsy and learning disabilities, the emphasis is increasingly on obtaining seizure control or, better still, elimination of seizures altogether. This can be to the detriment of behaviour, alertness, ability to learn motor skills and general well-being. Although the nature and frequency of seizures can be an indicator of a person's level of well-being, e.g. seizure frequency can increase when a person is coming down with an illness, nevertheless, medication effect should be balanced against seizure effect. This is not always easy to assess in children and young people with complex neurological impairments, refractory (difficult or resistant to treat) epilepsy and/or additional sensory and communication problems. Understanding how such children feel, whether they are nauseous, unwell or depressed needs skilful and astute observation carried out by family, carers and those involved with them on a daily basis. Measuring a person's quality of life in a clear and objective manner can provide structure to the observations and help us plan to improve areas that are weak or unsatisfactory for that person.

Such procedures are very useful when the child changes schools or the young person moves on to post-16 provision, leaves a school or moves into independent living accommodation. Kerr and Espie (1997) suggest an intervention system using a flow chart model once such areas of weakness have been established. Although a model originally designed for use with adults, it has relevance here (see Figure 7.1).

Ultimately the only way that families can learn to cope is by

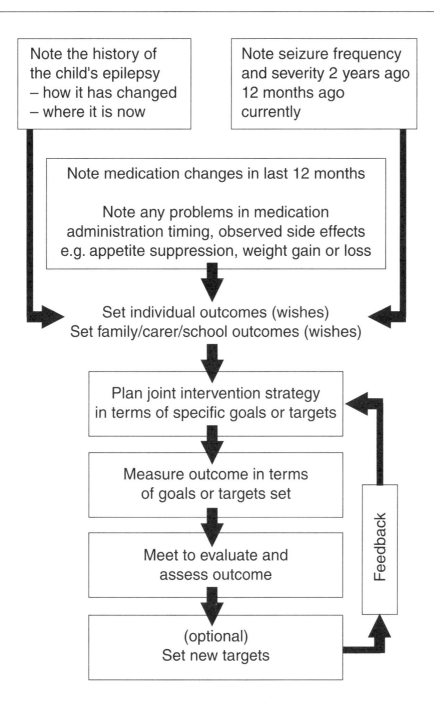

Figure 7.1 Quality of Life model applied to epilepsy – setting evidence based targets. Reproduced from Kerr, M. P. and Espie, C. A. (1997) 'Learning disability and epilepsy: towards common outcome measures', *Seizure*, 6, 331–6.

taking control of the situation in a way in which they feel comfortable. They need help first in mobilising those ways of handling feelings and events that have proved effective for them in the past. All strategies have costs and benefits – only the family has the right to define what is an acceptable balance for them.

In our experience, medical professionals generally accept parents taking an assertive stance. Many doctors in the Johnson and Thomson study said that they did not know what to say to parents because they were unaware of how the information would be received or how parents would cope with the information. Their sample showed that parents were far better able to cope than they were given credit for. What they found difficult was being given false reassurance or treated as though they were stupid!

It is essential that parents develop an understanding of the generality of the treatment that their child is likely to experience. Equipped with this knowledge, parents are better positioned to set in place coping mechanisms and strategies prior to an event, i.e. before the appointment at the EEG unit, rather than on arrival.

We also think that it would be good practice for schools to recognise the value of the coping strategies parents have developed. A simple informal meeting of parents, teachers and a person with medical knowledge (school nurse, medical officer, specialist epilepsy nurse, etc.) allows parents to pass on their knowledge and experiences. The school could ask questions about epilepsy and its implications and really begin to understand how it manifests itself in that particular child. Such active knowledge is vital if the child is to be given the opportunity to have a successful education. There would be a follow-up meeting scheduled for the end of each term allowing for both parents and school to test the effectiveness of the partnership generated.

It is also important to recognise that there may be wide cultural variations in the way in which epilepsy is perceived. Respecting such views (providing they do not conflict with effective management of the child's epilepsy) seems to us to be only reasonable – particularly as the medical profession has coined the term, 'cryptogenic' to mean 'I don't know the cause' in relation to a significant proportion of childhood epilepsies!

Quality of life means creating the conditions under which a child with epilepsy can be, as far as possible, the child they would have been without the epilepsy. If they are stronger in other ways because they have learned to cope with a certain adversity, all the better. What is unforgivable is to add to that adversity through ignorance, defensiveness or prejudice.

Useful Addresses/Internet Sites

These provide advice, information and in some instances, local support groups and networks for families, carers and those with epilepsy. One or two, such as the British Epilepsy Association, also provide databases for those wishing to undertake research on epilepsy and related subjects.

Epilepsy organisations

British Epilepsy Association
New Anstey House
Gate Way Drive
Weadon
Leeds
LS19 7XY
Tel: 0113 210 8800
Freephone helpline: 0808 800 5050
Email: *epilepsy@bea.org.uk*
www.epilepsy.org.uk
Epilepsy information on-line: *www.epilepsy.org.uk/info.html*

National Society for Epilepsy
Chesham Lane
Chalfont St Peter
Buckinghamshire
SL9 0RJ
Tel: 01494 601300
Helpline: 01494 601400
www.epilepsynse.org.uk

Epilepsy Action Scotland
National Headquarters
48 Govan Road
Glasgow
G51 1JL
Tel: 0141 427 4911
Helpline: 0141 427 5225
Email: *enquiries@epilepsyscotland.org.uk*
www.epilepsyscotland.org.uk

Folks
(Friends of Landau Kleffner syndrome)
3 Stone Buildings
Lincoln's Inn (ground floor)
London
WC2A 3XL
Tel: 0870 847 0707
Email: *101361.2530@compuserve.com*
www.bobjanet.demon.co.uk/lks/folks.html

Irish Epilepsy Association
249 Crumlin Road
Dublin 12
Eire
Tel: (00353) 1455 7500

Mersey Region Epilepsy Association
Glaxo Neurological Centre
Norton Street
Liverpool
L3 8LR
Tel: 0151 298 2666

Epilepsy Wales
15 Chester Street
St Asaph
Denbighshire
LL17 0RE
Tel: 01745 584444
Helpline: 08457 413774
Email: *office@epilepsy-wales.co.uk*
www.epilepsy-wales.co.uk

International League Against Epilepsy
Avenue Marcel Thiry 204
B-1200 Brussels
Belgium
Tel: +32 (0) 2 774 9547
www.ilae-epilepsy.org

International Bureau for Epilepsy
253 Crumlin Road
Dublin 12
Eire
Tel: (00353) 1456 0298
Email: *ibedublin:eircom.net*
www.ibe-epilepsy.org

Epilepsy Foundation of America
4351 Garden City Drive, 5th Floor
Landover
Maryland 20785
USA
Tel: 001 301 457 3700
Email: *ehargis@efa.org*
www.epilepsyfoundation.org

Epilepsy Canada
1470 Peel Street, Suite 745
Montreal
Quebec
H34 1T1
Canada
Tel: 001 514 845 7855
Email: *crepin@epilepsy.ca*
www.epilepsy.ca

As well as the addresses listed here, many regional neurology units have specialist epilepsy services. In some areas, larger primary care groups will run out-patient epilepsy clinics.

Assessment centres for epilepsy

David Lewis Centre
Mill Lane
Warford
Nr Alderley Edge
Cheshire
SK9 7UD
Tel: 01565 640000

King's College Hospital – Epilepsy Unit
De'crispigny Park
Denmark Hill
London
SE5 9ES
Tel: 020 7346 5379

Park Hospital for Children
Old Road
Headington
Oxford
OX3 7LQ
Tel: 01865 741717

Neurology Department
York District Hospital
Wiginton Road
York
YO3 7HE
Tel: 01904 725752

Schools for children with epilepsy

Most children are educated in mainstream or special schools in their locality. Children with more complicated epilepsies, or who have additional complex needs such as learning and behaviour disability conditions requiring high levels of medical supervision may need to be educated in residential or more specialised 'out-of-county' placements. Addresses of the main specialist residential schools are given below.

David Lewis School
Mill Lane
Warford
Nr Alderley Edge
Cheshire
SK9 7UD
Tel: 01565 640000

National Centre for Young People with Epilepsy
St Piers Lane
Lingfield
Surrey
HR7 6PW
Tel: 01342 832243

St Elizabeth's
South End
Bourne Lane
Much Hadden
Herts
SG10 6EW
Tel: 0127 984 3451

Information on syndromes and related subjects can be found on *www.findarticles.com*

Qualifications and Curriculum Authority
Email: *info@qca.org.uk*

Information on including all learners,
www.qca.org.uk/ca/inclusion/key_principles.asp

QCA Publications
PO Box 99
Sudbury
Suffolk CO10 2SN
Tel: 01787 884444
Email: *QCA@Prolog.uk.com*

Joint Council for General Qualifications
www.jcgq.org.uk

Copies of the (2001) Special Educational Needs Code of Practice are available from

DfES Publications
PO Box 5050
Sherwood Park
Annesley
Nottinghamshire
NG15 0DG
Tel: 0845 6022260
email: dfes@prolog.uk.com
DfES website: www.dfes.gov.uk

Information on inclusion can be found on
http://inclusion.ngfl.gov.uk

Other useful addresses/ Internet sites

Bibliography

Adams, C., Byers-Brown, B. and Edwards, M. (1997). *Developmental Disorders of Language*. London: Whurr.

American Psychiatric Association (1994). *Diagnostic Criteria from DSM-IV*. Washington: American Psychiatric Association.

Appleton, R. E. (1995) 'Drug treatment of paediatric epilepsy', in J. S. Duncan and J. Q. Gill (eds) *Lecture Notes for the 5th Epilepsy Teaching Weekend, Keble College, Oxford*. London: Ciba-Geigy Scientific Publications.

Appleton, R. and Gibbs, J. (1998) *Epilepsy in Childhood and Adolescence*. London: Dunitz.

Audit Commission (1997). *First Class Delivery: Improving Maternity Services in England and Wales*. Kent: Litho.

Austin, J. K. (1988) 'Childhood epilepsy: childhood adaptation and family resources'. *Journal of Child and Adolescent Psychiatric and Mental Health Nursing* **1**, 1, 18–24.

Bishop, D. V. M. and Rosenbloom, L. (1987) 'Classification of childhood language disorders', in W. Yule and M. Rutter (eds) *Language Development and Disorders*. Oxford: Blackwell Scientific Publications, in association with MacKeith Press.

Bjornaes, H. (1988) 'Consequences of severe epilepsy: psychological aspects'. *Acta Neurologica Scandinavia Supplement*, **117**, 28–33.

British Epilepsy Association (2001) http://www.epilepsy.org.uk/info.html.

Brodtkorb, E. (1999) 'Treatment of epilepsy in patients with intellectual disabilities: general principles and particular problems', in M. Sillampaa, L. Gram, S. I. Johannessen and T. Tomson (eds) *Epilepsy and Mental Retardation*. Petersfield: Wrightson Medical.

Brown, E. R. (1990) 'Inter-ictal cognitive changes in epilepsy'. *Seminars in Neurology* **11**(2), 167–74.

Brown, S., Betts, T., Chadwick, D. *et al.* (1993) 'An epilepsy needs document.' *Seizure*, 91–103.

Brown, S. W. (1994) 'A view from the playground', *Seizure* 3(Suppl. A), 11–15.

CARE Project (2000) *Epilepsy Alternative Seizure Record Chart Used in an Epilepsy Clinic.* Warford: David Lewis Centre (CARE Project).

Central Health Services Council (1956) *Report of the Sub-committee on the Medical Care of Epileptics.* London: HMSO.

Chadwick, D., Cartlidge, N. and Bates, D. (eds) (1989) *Medical Neurology.* Edinburgh: Churchill-Livingstone.

Childhood Epilepsy Survey (1994) *Making Waves.* London: TN AGB plc.

Collings, J. (1995) *Positive Action for Better Services: A survey of attitudes and experiences by the British Epilepsy Association.* Unpublished document.

Collings, J. (2000) *British Epilepsy Association Charter 2000: A report of a National Survey.* British Epilepsy Association (unpublished).

Commission on Classification and Terminology of the International League Against Epilepsy (1981) 'Proposal for revised clinical and electroencephalographic classification of epileptic seizures', *Epilepsia* **22**, 451–8.

Commission on Classification and Terminology of the International League Against Epilepsy (1985) 'Proposal for classification of epileptic seizures', *Epilepsia* **26**, 269–78.

Commission on Classification and Terminology of the International League Against Epilepsy (1989) 'Proposal for a revised classification of the epilepsies and epilepsy syndromes', *Epilepsia* **30**, 389–99.

Cromer, R. E. (1991) *Language and Thought in Normal and Handicapped Children.* Oxford: Blackwell.

Cull, C. and Goldstein, L. (1997) *The Child Psychologist's Handbook of Epilepsy Assessment and Management.* London: Routledge.

Department for Education and Employment (DfEE) (1994a) *Code of Practice on the Identification and Assessment of Pupils with Special Educational Needs.* London: DfEE.

Department for Education and Employment (DfEE) (1994b) *Special Educational Needs – a guide for parents.* London: DfEE.

Department for Education and Employment (DfEE) (1997a) *Excellence for All Children.* London: The Stationery Office.

Department for Education and Employment (DfEE) (1997b) *Excellence in Schools.* London: DfEE.

Department for Education and Employment (DfEE) (1998) *Meeting Special Educational Needs: A Programme for Action.* London: DfEE.

Department for Education and Employment (DfEE)(1999) *The National Curriculum*. London: DfEE.

Department for Education and Skills (DfES) (2001) *The Revised Code of Practice on the Identification and Assessment of Pupils with Special Educational Needs*. London: The Stationery Office.

Department of Education and Science (DES) (1978) *Special Educational Needs* (The Warnock Report). London: HMSO.

Department of Education and Science (DES) (1981) *Education Act 1981*. London: HMSO.

Department of Health (DoH) (1996) *Supporting Pupils with Medical Needs: A good practice guide*. London: DoH.

Education Act 1996: Elizabeth II. Chapter 56. Part IV. London: HMSO.

Education Act 1997: Elizabeth II. Chapter 44, Part IV, Chapter I, Section 26. London: The Stationery Office.

Emblem, B., Leonard, J., Dale, E., Redmond, J. and Bowes, R. (1998) 'The challenge of Class Six', in D. Hewett (ed.) *Challenging Behaviour: Principles and Practices*, 50–68. London: David Fulton Publishers.

Emerson, E., McGill, P. and Mansell, J. (eds) (1994) *Severe Learning Disabilities and Challenging Behaviours*. London: Chapman and Hall.

Engel, J. (2001) 'ILAE Commission Report: a proposed diagnostic scheme for people with epileptic seizures and with epilepsy. Report of the ILAE Task Force on Classification and Terminology'. *Epilesia* **42**(6), 1–8.

Espie, C., Kerr, M., Paul, A. *et al.* (1997) 'Learning disability and epilepsy: outcome measures and position statement on development priorities', *Seizure* **6**, 337–50.

Ford, C. A., Gibson, P. and Dreifuss, F. E. (1983) 'Psychosocial consideration in childhood epilepsy', in F. E. Dreifus, *Paediatric Epileptology* (pp 277–95) Boston: John Wright, PSG, pp. 277–95.

Fowler, M. (1997) 'Neuropsychological and cognitive assessment of children with epilepsy', in C. Cull and L. Goldstein (eds) *The Child Psychologist's Handbook of Epilepsy Assessment and Management*. London: Routledge, pp. 149–65.

Freeman, J. M., Vinning, E. P. G. and Pillas, D. J. (1997) *Seizures and Epilepsy in Childhood, A Guide for Parents*. Baltimore, MD: Johns Hopkins Press.

Gallassi, R., Moreale, A., Lorusso, S. *et al.* (1988) 'Epilepsy presenting as memory disturbance', *Epilepsia* **20**(5), 524–9.

Gilberg, C. and O'Brien, G.(eds) (2000)*Developmental Disability and Behaviour*. London: MacKeith Press.

Hagerman, R. J., Schriemer, R. A., Kemper, M. B. *et al.* (1989) 'Longitudinal IQ changes in Fragile X males'. *Americal Journal of Medical Genetics*, **33**, 513–18.

Haynes, C. and Naidoo, C. (1991) 'Children with specific speech and language impairments'. *Clinics in Developmental Medicine*, 119. London: MacKeith Press.

Hermann, B. P. (1991) 'Contribution of traditional assessment procedures to our understanding of the neuropsychology of epilepsy', in W. E. Dodson, M. Kinsborne and B. Hilthrunner (eds) *Assessment of Cognitive Function in Epilepsy*. New York: DEMOS.

Hewett, D. (ed.) (1998) *Challenging Behaviour: Principles and Practices*. London: David Fulton Publishers.

Hewett, D. (ed.) (2000) *Challenging Behaviour: Principles and Practices*, 2nd edn. London: David Fulton Publishers.

HMSO (1991) *Population Estimates (England and Wales)*, Office of Population Census and Surveys. London: HMSO.

Holdsworth, L. and Whitmore, K. (1974) 'A study of children with epilepsy attending ordinary schools. II. Information and attitudes held by teachers', *Developmental Medicine and Child Neurology* **16**, 759–65.

Hopkins, A. and Appleton, R. (1996) *Epilepsy: the facts*. Oxford: Oxford University Press.

Jackson, J. H. (1873) 'On the anatomical, physiological and pathological investigation of epilepsies, West Riding Lunatic Asylum Medical Report 3:35', in J. Taylor (ed.) *Selected Writing of John Hughlings Jackson*, 90–111. Sevenoaks: Hodder and Stoughton.

Janz, D. and Waltz, S. (1994) 'Juvenile myoclonic epilepsy with absences', in J. S. Duncan and C. P. Panayiotopoulos (eds) *Typical Absences and Related Epileptic Syndromes*. London: Churchill-Livingstone.

Johnson, M. C. and Thomas, L. (1998) The Code of Practice on the Identification and Assessment of Special Educational Needs (SEN) and Pupils with an Epileptic Condition. Manchester: Manchester Metropolitan University (unpublished).

Kerr, M. (1999) 'Epilepsy and learning disability', in J. S. Duncan and J. E. Small (eds) *Epilepsy: from science to patient*. Edenbridge: Meritus Communications for International League Against Epilepsy.

Kerr, M. P. and Espie, C. A. (1997) 'Learning disability and epilepsy I: towards common outcome measures'. *Seizure* 6: 331–6.

Lacey, P. (2001) Support Partnerships: Collaboration in Action. London: David Fulton Publishers.

Lechtenberg, R. (1984) *Epilepsy and the Family*. Harvard University Press.

Lees, J. (1993) *Children with Acquired Aphasias*. London: Whurr.

Lees, J. and Neville, B. G. R. (1990) 'Acquired aphasia in childhood: case studies of five children', *Aphasiology* **4**, 463–78.

Margalit, M. and Heiman, T. (1986) 'Anxiety and self-dissatisfaction in epileptic children'. *International Journal of Social Psychiatry* **29**(3), 220–4.

Mattthews, W. S., Barabas, G. and Ferrari, M. (1982) 'Emotional concomitants of childhood epilepsy'. *Epilepsia* **23**, 671–81.

Neville, B., Burch, V., Cross, H. and Lees, J. (2000) 'Behavioural Aspects of Landau-Kleffner Syndrome', in C. Gillberg and G. O'Brien, *Developmental Disability and Behaviour*. Cambridge: Cambridge University Press, pp. 56–63.

Oxbury, J., Polkey, C. and Du Chowny, M. (2000) *Intractable Focal Epilepsy*. London: W. B. Saunders.

Parkinson, G. (1999) *Complex Epilepsy and Childhood Language Disability*. Unpublished PhD, Manchester Metropolitan University.

Picirilli, M., Pattrizia, S. A., Sciama, D. *et al.* (1994) 'Attention problems in epilepsy: possible significance of the epileptogenic focus', *Epilepsia* **35**(5), 1091–6.

Qualifications and Curriculum Authority (QCA) (1997) *Assessment and Reporting Arrangements at Key Stage 2* (ref QCA 97/002). London: QCA/DfEE.

Qualifications and Curriculum Authority (QCA) (2000) *Including All Learners*. London: QCA/DfEE.

Richardson, S. A., Koller, H. and Katz, M. (1981) 'A functional classification of seizures and their distribution in a mentally retarded population', *American Journal of Mental Deficiency* **85**, 457–66.

Robinson, R. J. (1987) 'The causes of language disorder introduction and overview', *Proceedings of the First International Symposium of Specific Speech and Language Disorders*. Reading: Afasic.

Robinson, R. J. (1991) 'Causes and associations of severe and persistent specific speech and language disorders in childhood'. *Developmental Medicine and Child Neurology* **33**(11), 943–62.

Rogan, P. J. (1992) *Epilepsy: A Teacher's Handbook*. Oxford: Alden Press.

Rutter, M. (1978) 'Diagnosis and definition', in M. Rutter and E. Schapler (eds) *Autism: A Re-Appraisal of Concepts and Treatment*. New York: Plenum Press.

Scrambler, G. (1990) 'Social factors and quality of care in epilepsy', in *Quality of Life and Quality of Care in Epilepsy*. London: Royal Society of Medicine.

Sillanpaa, M. (1983) 'Social functioning and seizure status of young adults with onset of epilepsy in childhood', *Acts Neurologica Scandinavica* **68**(Suppl. 96), 1–81.

Simensson, R. J., Edmonson, R., Smith, T. *et al.* (1995) 'Family involvement in multi-disciplinary team evaluation: professional and parent perspectives', *Childcare, Health and Development* **21**(3), 199–215.

Squires, J. K., Nickel, R. and Bricker, D. (1990) 'Use of parent completed development questionnaire for child find and screening. Infant and young children', *Infant and Young Children* **3**, 46–57.

Steffenberg, S., Gilbert, C. and Steffenberg, U. (1996) 'Psychiatric disorders in children and adolescents with mental retardation and active epilepsy', *Archives of Neurology* **53**, 904–12.

Stores, G. (1979) 'The schoolchild with epilepsy', *School Psychology International*, 17–23.

Taylor, D. C. (1993) 'Epilepsy as a chronic sickness', in J. Engel, Jnr (ed.) *Surgical Treatment of the Epilepsies*. New York: Raven Press.

Vance, M. (1991) 'Educational and therapeutic approaches used with a child presenting with acquired aphasia with convulsive disorder (Landau-Kleffner syndrome)', *Child Language Teaching and Therapy* **7**, 41–60.

Walker, M. and Shorvon, S. (1999) *The British Medical Association Family Doctor Guide to Epilepsy*. London: Dorling Kindersley.

Walton, J. (1985) *Braine's Diseases of the Nervous System*. Oxford: Oxford University Press.

Williamson, P. D., French, J. A., Thadam, V. M. *et al.* (1993) 'Characteristics of medial temporal lobe epilepsy, II. inter-ictal and ictal encephalography, neuropsychological testing, neuroimaging, surgical results and pathology'. *Annals of Neuropsychology* **34**, 781–7.

Wolfensberger, W., Thomas, S. and Garson, G. (1996) 'Some of the universal "good things in life" which the implementation of social role valorisation can be expected to make more accessible to devalued people'. *Social Role Valorisation*, **2**(2), 12–14.

Ziegler, R. C. (1981) 'Impairments of control and competence in epileptic children and their families'. *Epilepsia* **22**(3), 339–46.

Index

absence seizures 7
  schooling 46–7
access to curriculum 58
  outdoor pursuits 65–7
  PE and games 65–7
  practical subjects 64–5
adolescence, impact on epilepsy 17–19
ambulatory monitoring 5
anti-epileptic drugs 10–17
assessment 22
attention control 25
atonic seizures 7

behaviour 71–2
  assessment of 71–2
  differentiating from seizure 70
  difficulties 68–81
  intervention strategies 73, 75–6
  prevention of over-arousal 74
benign childhood epilepsy 9
benign rolandic epilepsy 88
brain
  electrical activity 1
  imaging tests 4
  scans 6
  specific investigations 4–6
  surgery 16
British Epilepsy Association 30

causes
  epilepsy 3
  seizures 3
children
  absences 53
  academic performance 59
  parenting 51–2
classification
  ILAE system 9
  seizures 9
  syndromes 8, 9
classroom assistants see learning
  support assistants 29
clinics see services, support services
clonic seizures 7
Code of Practice 41–4
cognitive assessment 22
communication see language
complex partial seizures 7, 8
computerised tomography (CT) 4
continuous epilepsy see status
  epilepticus
convulsions see seizures
cryptogenic epilepsies 4
CSWS 89–90
CT see computerised tomography
curriculum access 58–67

definition of epilepsy 1
diabetes 1

diagnosis 4, 5
Down's syndrome 91
drug treatments
  knowledge of effects 49–51
  parents' comments 49

education, implications 39
educational psychologist 29
  assessment of cognitive ability 29
  evidence for examinations 60–5
  role in SEN procedure 70
electrical status in slow-wave sleep
  (ESES) see CSWS
electroencephalography (EEG) in
  diagnosis of epilepsy 4–6
epilepsy
  causes 3
  classification 3
  cryptogenic 3, 4
  diagnosis 3, 4
  definition 1
  education of teachers 57
  family, implications for 30–1
  genetics 19–21
  liaison nurse 31
  localisation related 9
  management in schools 48–9, 92
  symptomatic 4, 9
examinations and assessments 62–4

family 30–1
first-aid treatment 12, 66
fits see seizures
focal epilepsies 2
Fragile X syndrome 92
frontal lobe epilepsy 26

general practitioner 31
genetics 19–21
glossary ix–xii
'grand mal seizures' see tonic-clonic
  seizures 7

hereditory factors see genetics 19–21
hypsarrhythmia, see West syndrome

idiopathic epilepsies 4
imaging 4
information 44–5
  addresses 105–9
inherited factors see genetics
intelligence testing 25, 28
internet sites 105–9
investigations 4, 33–4

Joint Council for General Qualifications
  61
juvenile myoclonic epilepsies 20

Landau-Kleffner syndrome 90–2

language problems 82–3
  epilepsy related factors 83–4
  medication effect 86–7
  types of seizures 84–6
learning difficulties 102
learning support assistants (LSAs) 29
Lennox-Gastaut syndrome 89
light induced seizures
  see photosensitivity
localisation related epilepsies see ILAE
  classification
  language disability 88

magnetic resonance imaging (MRI)
  33–4
medication effect 86
memory 27
migraine 1

over-protection 99–100

parents see family 30–1
photosensitivity 19
physical education (PE) 65–7
practical subjects 64–5

Qualifications and Curriculum
  Authority (QCA) 61–2
quality of life 95–104

Rasmussen's syndrome 90
Rett syndrome 91
risk assessment 100

school
  academic subjects 59–61
  negative perceptions of 56
  positive perceptions of 56–7
  SENCO 29
seizures
  classification 9
  management 34–7
  recording frequency charts 13–15
  treatment 10–17
sleep, continuous spike-waves in slow-
  wave sleep see CSWS
social aspects of living with epilepsy
  77–81
status epilepticus 10
surgery 16
swimming 66
symptomatic epilepsies 4

temporal lobe epilepsy (TLE) 9
  testing functions in TLE 26
tonic seizures 7
tonic-clonic seizures 7
tuberous sclerosis 91

West syndrome 89